What people are saying about

Befuddled

David Birch has produced a series of amusing and informative sketches of some great philosophers and thinkers. It is a stimulating and very enjoyable romp.
Stephen Law, philosopher and author

Rich and beautiful, these stories educate and enchant in equal measure. This is a book that people of all ages would prosper from.
Andy West, author of *The Life Inside: A Memoir of Prison, Family and Philosophy*

Befuddled

The Lives & Legends of
Ancient Philosophers

Befuddled

The Lives & Legends of Ancient Philosophers

David Birch

IFF
BOOKS

Winchester, UK
Washington, USA

JOHN HUNT PUBLISHING

First published by iff Books, 2023
iff Books is an imprint of John Hunt Publishing Ltd., No. 3 East Street, Alresford,
Hampshire SO24 9EE, UK
office@jhpbooks.com
www.johnhuntpublishing.com
www.iff-books.com

For distributor details and how to order please visit the 'Ordering' section on our website.

Text copyright: David Birch 2022

ISBN: 978 1 78904 826 1
978 1 78904 827 8 (ebook)
Library of Congress Control Number: 2022930125

A CIP catalogue record for this book is available from the British Library.

Design: Matthew Greenfield

UK: Printed and bound by CPI Group (UK) Ltd, Croydon, CR0 4YY
Printed in North America by CPI GPS partners

We operate a distinctive and ethical publishing philosophy in
all areas of our business, from our global network of authors to
production and worldwide distribution.

Contents

Other Titles by this Author

Pandora's Book: 401 Philosophical Questions to
Help You Lose Your Mind (with answers)
ISBN: 978 1 78904 571 0

Thinking Beans: A Year of Classroom Philosophy Lessons
ISBN: 978 1 90890 104 0

Provocations: Philosophy for Secondary School
ISBN: 978 1 78583 368 7

For a darling creature named Sebastian

Introduction

I'll be frank, philosophy is for freaks. The stories in this book prove it. What other conclusion can one reasonably draw when faced with tales of public urination, volcano jumping and bean phobia? But it's hardly surprising. Just imagine, living a life of perpetual befuddlement! Yet that's what they do. It's what makes them philosophers. If human zoos existed, the pen description for these creatures would explain:

> Forever perplexed, the philosopher spends its
> days lost in contemplation.

WARNING

Avoid asking questions – its answers will
only leave you more confused.

Every creature has its habitat and philosophers are no different. Fish spend their days suspended in water. Birds, the air. Philosophers, alternatively, inhabit puzzles, perplexities and problems. And where fish have fins to swim and birds wings to fly, philosophers use thoughts to ride the currents of their confusion. Like fins and wings, philosophers' thoughts carry them to places that many of us have never been. This is why we ought to celebrate and not castigate them for being freaks. In their strangeness and difference freaks can accomplish wondrous things.

So, dear reader, if you love to question and are often confused, you may well be a philosopher-freak. Though, to be clear, the philosopher's confusion is of a special kind. They don't spend their lives baffled by ordinary matters such as where they left their phone or why their train was delayed. These

1

ordinary confusions are caused by the problems of everyday life. Philosophical confusions, on the other hand, are caused by extraordinary moments.

Imagine that you're sitting in a car mindlessly watching the houses go by. This is an ordinary experience. But now something strange happens: you stop seeing the passing houses and start to see yourself watching the passing houses. It's as though you can see yourself from the outside, as though you're no longer in the car but watching yourself in the car. You've somehow left yourself behind. And in this moment, as you see yourself sitting there, you wonder: *Who am I? What am I?*

Befuddlement has seized you! Your ordinary experience has been disrupted by an extraordinary perspective, and from this a baffling question has suddenly appeared. But this isn't the end of the matter. Philosophical confusion rapidly grows and expands. From your one question many more arise.

When did I begin? Was it with my first heartbeat, first breath or first thought? If I ask someone who I am, they will say my name, but a name is only a sound, so am I only a sound? What does that sound refer to? Is it my mind? Or my body? Or my life? Does it refer to anything at all?!

This is philosophical confusion. It happens when ordinary life is suddenly ruptured by extraordinary moments, moments that give rise to the strangest questions. Ordinarily other people ask us who we are, we don't ask ourselves. Ordinarily we ask what the time is, not what time itself is. And ordinarily we might ask to borrow someone's clothes, but it rarely occurs to us to ask whether we can borrow their bodies. These latter questions are philosophical questions. We don't invent or go looking for them. They find us in those bizarre moments when our ordinary lives are turned inside out.

Though it's understandable to be disconcerted by these extraordinary questions, philosophers are thrilled by them. They find befuddlement exhilarating. This is because it unleashes an awesome power, a power we all possess – a power *you* possess. This is the power of thinking.

Thinking is an almighty force, one more powerful than the sun and sea combined. The sea, you see, can only ever react. The tide is a reaction to gravity. The waves are a reaction to wind. And people are similar, we often just react. If someone pushes you, you might react by pushing them back. If you are scolded by an authority figure, you might react by feeling guilty or indignant. Thinking, however, stops us merely reacting. It allows us to question what is happening and why it is happening. By thinking we might, for instance, realise that we have no reason to feel guilty, that we did nothing wrong. By thinking a little more we might even start to believe that everyone is always doing what they believe is right, therefore no one should feel guilty for anything (Socrates, who we'll look at in chapter 6, thought something similar to this).

Consider the philosopher Diogenes (another philosopher we'll look at). He was a social outcast. No one liked him. If he'd simply reacted to this rejection, he would've spent his entire life sad. But he didn't.

One day while he was dining alone he noticed a mouse scurrying about after his crumbs. He noticed how content the mouse was despite possessing so little, and having no status, and being so unloved. This led Diogenes to pose an extraordinary question. Rather than simply ask the ordinary reactive question, *Why does no one like me?* he asked himself, *Is it better to be liked or free?*

In this extraordinary moment, this moment of seeing a lowly mouse as an inspiration rather than a pest, he became befuddled about why humans exhaust so much time and energy trying to fit in, and this befuddlement sent his mind soaring. He looked at the mouse and suddenly saw an alternative way of living, a different world in which he, like a mouse, would simply follow his own natural inclinations, freeing himself from the wish to please others and the burden to act normally.

Diogenes's thoughts allowed him to see new forms of life, new worlds of possibility, and this is why thinking is so powerful, and why philosophers are so excited by it. Despite the awesomeness of the sun, it cannot burn purple or darken its glow. It lacks the power. And despite the might of the sea, it cannot still the march of its waves. The sun and sea are both stuck as they are. But with the power of thinking you can recreate and change the world.

Those changes, however, are entirely unpredictable. We cannot know where our thoughts are going to take us, or what we might end up believing, or disbelieving. To allow yourself to think is rather like launching yourself into a tornado. You have to let yourself get carried away.

This is the bizarre thing about thinking: though it is a power we all possess, it is a power over which we have no power. Philosophical thoughts are thoughts you cannot control. They are not constrained by rules or bound by what is normal. If you allow them, they will probe, explode, shatter and shake everything you thought you once knew.

In this book we are going to look at stories from the biographies of ancient philosophers, of those curious individuals who devoted their lives to befuddlement, to strange questions and extraordinary thoughts. These individuals didn't just think about philosophy, they lived it. And as we shall discover, to live a life animated by befuddlement is an experiment that leads to rather peculiar and startling results.

Having lived thousands of years ago it is not always possible to know what really happened. Some of the stories may seem unbelievable and some are most certainly legends rather than facts. Nevertheless, though these stories may not always be true, they are always interesting. And that is the real point of this book: to present strange stories and curious ideas so that you may start your own extraordinary explorations, discover your own powers of thought, and experience for yourself the freaky thrills of befuddlement.

1

Pythagoras

Φ *Pronunciation* Pie-thag-a-russ
Φ *Time* 570-480 BCE
Φ *Born* Samos (Greece)
Φ *Quote* 'Do not pee facing the sun.'

Pythagoras had a great thirst for travel. It was an appetite he was unusually adept at satisfying due to his handy ability to be in different places at the same time. He could, for instance, confabulate with the philosophers on Crete while simultaneously learning the secrets of the magi in Iran. With this unbelievable talent he quickly and expertly acquired a rich and varied education. This, indeed, was the very reason he wanted to travel. He was on a quest of befuddlement, a journey for knowledge and understanding. He wished to discover the truths of existence, life, the world, reality – everything.

But when he returned to his native Samos after many years of exploration he was aggrieved to discover that the island was under the rule of a tyrant named Polycrates. For Pythagoras this was a disaster. A philosopher can no more live without freedom than a fire can burn without oxygen. And so he left. He travelled to Croton in Italy and there pursued his ongoing quest for knowledge and understanding.

Pythagoras's ideas, and his dazzling ability to express them, were so enthralling that in Croton he started to amass followers. In fact, he was so spellbinding a speaker that wild animals would do as he asked. He once convinced a bloodthirsty bear to become a vegetarian. Another time he managed to persuade an ox to refrain from eating beans (he found beans particularly bothersome, as we shall see).

His fame and popularity continued to grow – even to the extent that rivers would greet him as he crossed them – and it wasn't long before he found that he had unwittingly become the leader of a commune. Pythagorean pilgrims would travel for hundreds of miles to listen to his teachings, and they would seldom leave.

As more pilgrims arrived and fewer left the commune grew unsustainably large. In order to quell the numbers Pythagoras made the initiation process testing enough to filter out those who lacked a genuine commitment to his ideas. For the first five years his followers were required to live in total silence. Moreover, they were not permitted to see him and could only attend his lectures blindfolded.

Once welcomed into the commune his disciples were required to hand over all of their possessions to the group. Pythagoras believed that a friend is an extension of ourselves, and if I am you, it follows that what's mine is yours. Accordingly, his followers shared everything, from beds to showers to toothbrushes.

Let's try to imagine one of his lectures. See him standing before us in the warm Mediterranean sun, balancing on a barrel, dressed in a pure white robe.

'Do not pray for yourselves for you do not know what you need,' he exclaims.

'Very wise,' the crowd murmur.

'And do not pee facing the sun,' he continues.

'Huh? Why do you think we're not supposed to pee facing the sun?' a man near us whispers to his friend.

'Would you pee facing your mother?' the friend replies.

'That's disgusting!'

'Well there you go.'

'But the sun ain't my mother.'

'It's a question of respect.'

'Respect the sun! What a load of –'

'Pipe down. He's saying something about beans.'

'Never eat beans! Do not even touch them,' Pythagoras

declares.

'Why must we not eat beans, master?' another follower calls out. 'I like beans.'

'Should we preserve our self-control in all things?'

'Yes, master.'

'And what happens to the fool who eats beans?'

'He farts, master.'

'And how do people react when they hear farts?'

'They laugh, master.'

'And so you see, one sin begets another. An outburst of gas leads to an outburst of mirth. We must cease all outbursts.'

'I see, master.'

He now holds up a confused puppy.

'This is my uncle, treat him kindly.'

'How can it be your uncle, master? It's a dog.'

'If I, Pythagoras, climbed into this barrel, would you say I *was* a barrel?'

'No, master, I'd say that you was *in* a barrel.'

'Likewise, though my uncle is inside a dog, he is not a dog. Do not mistake the garments for he who wears them.'

'Master, by what misfortune did your uncle get himself stuck in a dog?'

'By death.'

'Oh dear.'

'My dear followers, death is only a temporary misfortune. Do not fear it.'

You see, Pythagoras believed that our souls are eternal and distinct from our mortal bodies (a view known as dualism). Once your body dies the soul passes into a new body. These beliefs in dualism and reincarnation (also called metempsychosis) inspired Pythagoras to reject the norms of the time by admitting women into his commune. Women then were seen as unworthy of intellectual or spiritual pursuits. Their place was thought be in the home. But since sex is a feature of the body and not the soul, Pythagoras did not believe we could be separated into male and female. These categories merely describe our temporary abodes and do not characterise our true, eternal nature.

And just as Pythagoras did not think of himself as male or female, nor did he think of himself as human. Our human form is as temporary as our sex. In the next life you may well inhabit anything from a mighty whale to a lowly tick. You may have even been these creatures before. This is why Pythagoras refrained from eating meat: to eat a living creature is an act of cannibalism for you are consuming your own kind, another soul.

He once encountered a couple of fishermen hauling their bulging nets into a boat and yelled from the shore predicting the number of fish they had caught. The men shouted back that if he was right they would do whatever he wished. They were therefore alarmed to find that his number was accurate.

How did Pythagoras exercise this wish? He told the fishermen to return the fish to the sea. In that one net alone there may have been dozens of wives, husbands, children and friends from former lives. The prospect of their suffocation was unbearable to him.

For Pythagoras these ideas about metempsychosis were not merely theoretical. He was blessed with vivid memories of his former lives, even his plant lives. Just as he enjoined his followers to avoid meat, he also commanded them not to destroy or harm plants. Our kinship lies not only with animals but with every living thing.

Pythagoras didn't only develop ideas about our souls and life and death. Like many ancient philosophers he was eager to discover what the universe was fundamentally made of. This is an area of philosophy called ontology. Of all the ancient philosophers Pythagoras's ontology was perhaps the strangest.

Whereas other philosophers thought that the universe was

made out of some sort of physical substance, something we can see or touch, like fire or water, Pythagoras claimed that the universe was built from something both invisible and intangible: numbers. They are the fundamental stuff of existence. They are everywhere and everything. Justice, for instance, is based on the numerical relation of equality, for acting justly means treating people equally.

It was through studying the relationships between musical notes that he first glimpsed the universe's numerical essence. He wanted to understand why certain notes played in sequence created euphonious melodies and was astonished to discover that the intervals between those notes correlated to mathematical ratios. One such interval consists of two notes where one string is half the length of the other. This interval, which is a ratio of 2/1, is known as an octave. Other pleasing intervals, such as fifths (playing, say, C and G), are produced when one string is a third longer than the other. This is therefore expressed as the ratio 3/2.

Pythagoras concluded that the beauty of music arises from these numerical relationships. When we experience the pleasure of a symphony or song we are unconsciously attuned to an exquisite mathematical structure. But these structures are not confined to instruments such as lyres and organs. The whole universe is suffused with cosmic harmonies.

Pythagoras claimed that the orbiting planets each produce their own distinctive notes. These combine to fill the heavens with celestial music: the universe is singing. Unlike Pythagoras, however, most of us are deaf to its song because we have grown accustomed to it. We are unable to hear the music because we have never not heard it.

These mathematical relationships structure everything. The movements and motions of the universe are essentially the movements and motions of numbers. It was the wish to study and unearth such secrets that made Pythagoras's pilgrims so passionate in their longing to join the commune. Passion, however, can quickly, and destructively, lead to conflict – a fact which became all too clear when a pilgrim who had been denied entry to the commune exacted revenge by burning down the communal house.

Pythagoras managed to escape the fire. Since he despised anger and believed that we ought to treat every enemy as a potential friend, he was not predisposed to fight back (also, he was 90 years old by this point) and so he fled, slowly. Were it not for a most singular obstacle he might have gotten away, but he was thwarted, stopped in his tracks, by his greatest foe: the pernicious bean.

For years he had taught his followers not to touch, let alone eat, beans. With a whole field of them now at his feet he was forced to decide what was more important to him: his life or his teachings. He swiftly pondered this dilemma and concluded that living in accordance with

11

his principles must also mean dying in accordance with them, and so, with the sound of his assailant's footsteps steadily approaching, he fell to his knees, closed his eyes and waited, and waited, and then it was finished. Face down in the dirt, he spent his final flickering moments watching the soil gulp the blood that drained out of his throat.

Despite Pythagoras's death his disciples continued to live by his rules and study his theories. Within mathematics they discovered and examined a special category of numbers which we now call prime numbers. They also noted and explored the interesting differences between odd and even numbers. Turning to astronomy, they expanded on Pythagoras's discoveries that the earth was not the centre of the universe and that the moon's glow was the reflected light of the sun. They even started to wonder about the existence of extraterrestrial life, speculating that the moon was populated by creatures stronger, taller and more beautiful than humans.

During the middle of the 5th century BCE there were a series of anti-Pythagorean attacks and once again the commune was torched. Unfortunately, this time most of the Pythagoreans were burnt alive. The movement didn't survive much longer and by the end of the 4th century BCE it had disappeared completely.

2

Heraclitus

Φ *Pronunciation* Hair-a-cly-tuss
Φ *Time* 540-480 BCE
Φ *Born* Ephesus (Turkey)
Φ *Quote* 'War is father of all and king of all.'

Heraclitus died smothered in poo. Yes, poo.

How did so great a philosopher come to so smelly an end? Well, in order to understand the circumstances of his death we must start by considering the frustrations of his life.

Heraclitus had a restless mind that constantly fizzed with questions and ideas. The people of Ephesus (his hometown), however, were simpletons and dullards. It was impossible to discuss anything of interest with them. They were more interested in stuffing their faces with food than exercising their minds.

Heraclitus couldn't bear their stupidity. If he asked them what controlled the universe, they would say the gods. If he then asked them how they knew this, they would cite the poets. And if he asked how the poets knew, they would explain that someone must have told them. And if he asked how that person knew, they would conclude that he must have heard it in a poem.

When faced with befuddling questions they simply and blindly believed what they had been taught or went along with what everyone else said. If you tried to determine the reason for these beliefs, you'd find yourself trapped in an endless circle of stupidity. Heraclitus often lost his patience with the Ephesians. He'd yell at them to open their eyes, use their senses, explore, look, think, ignore the opinions of the crowd.

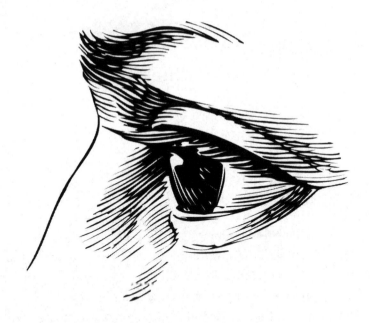

But they didn't listen. The only way they would stop following the crowd is if the crowd told them they ought to.

He felt isolated. He longed for interesting conversations. He wanted to discuss the nature of the world and existence, but the Ephesians merely lived in their own private dream-worlds, refusing to open their eyes and look at the world around them. 'Wake up!' he would shout at them. 'Wake up, you sleeping fools!'

Though he had been in line to become king he refused the throne. He did not want to waste his life ruling over idiots. The older and angrier he grew the more time he spent in the company of children, playing childish games such as hopscotch. Children's capacity for curiosity, wonder and idiosyncratic thought was a merciful antidote to the tedium of adult conversation.

One day the Ephesians sought his help to devise their laws and found him standing with a lampshade on his head.

'Heraclitus, the city needs you,' they said. He was unresponsive. 'Heraclitus?'

'Hush!'

'What was that?'

'You'll reveal my hiding place,' he whispered.

'Heraclitus, we sorely need your guidance and wisdom.'

'Can't help you, sorry, I'm just a lamp.'

Worried that they had in fact mistaken a lamp for a philosopher, the simple Ephesians tried to switch him on.

'Get your hands off me!' he shrieked, while blindly throwing punches at the air around him.

Shortly after this confrontation he gave up on Ephesus altogether. He had tried to share his ideas with the locals, but they either refused to listen or reacted with hostility. 'Why try to reason with animals?' he would say to himself. 'Dogs simply bark at what is unfamiliar.'

And so he set off from his hometown to live in the mountains. But the profound loneliness left him feeling tired and despondent, and he was never able to summon the energy to complete his philosophical texts. Without an audience to read his work he found writing pointless.

His weariness was made worse by the lack of sustenance in the mountains. Eventually his low-protein diet of grass and herbs left him suffering from dropsy (oedema), a condition that makes one's legs and feet swell with water.

He hobbled down from the mountains to consult the city's doctors, but they were unable (or unwilling) to cure his condition. Since heat leads to the annihilation of water (via evaporation) he reasoned that lying in the sun might serve as a remedy. To avoid sunburn he smeared bovine excrement (cowpats) over his body and lay on the ground exposed to the sweltering sun. It proved a costly cure.

By the next morning his suffering, and sadly his life, had come to an end. Where an onlooker would have seen a supine philosopher at dusk, at dawn there instead lay a half-eaten carcass at the mercy of scavenging dogs.

(Don't let the canine indignity bother you. Heraclitus believed that a body without a soul is mere refuse and would therefore have said that his corpse deserved no greater respect than the cowpats it was caked in.)

This, of course, is not the whole story of Heraclitus. He was not merely a cantankerous recluse but a philosopher. His life was lived in ideas. What were those ideas? To what heights and what depths did his restless mind take him? To answer these questions we first need to ask what it was that befuddled him.

Heraclitus found himself perplexed by events and incidents that most of us scarcely ever stop to think about. For instance, when we go to sleep it is night, but when we wake up it is morning. We then we go about our day without stopping to think about this curious change. For Heraclitus, however, such seemingly ordinary events were staggeringly bizarre. He was fascinated by the night's daily death and would wake up every morning in a fit of confusion. Had the night disappeared? Had it ceased to exist? Was it somehow in hiding?

The ancient Greek poet Hesiod believed that Day and Night were separate goddesses, Hemera and Nyx, who took turns ruling over the earth. According to Hesiod we go to sleep during Nyx's shift and wake at the start of Hemera's. Heraclitus, however, saw this as a perfect illustration of why we shouldn't trust the wisdom of poets or defer to the intelligence of other thinkers. He thought Hesiod was a fool.

According to Heraclitus night and day are not distinct entities; rather, they flow into and *become* each other. The day is not replaced by the night, it *becomes* the night, just as the night is not replaced by the day but *becomes* the day. The night dies to become something new, to transform into its opposite.

Heraclitus believed that this bizarre tendency of the night to transform into an opposite state (a process known as enantiodromia) revealed the tendency of all things. Everything is in a constant process of becoming its opposite. And this is why he thought that Homer, author of the *Iliad*, was another poetical fool, for in that poem Homer had the warrior Achilles express the wish that war and strife would disappear from the world. Homer had failed to realise that without war, without the quest for domination between opposing states, the world would perish.

To exist is to be part of an endless wave of destruction and creation. Nothing is still. Everything is changing, forever becoming what it is not. There is, for instance, no such thing as being purely young, or purely awake, or purely alive. We cannot be what we are without becoming what we are not: to be young is to be aging, to be awake is to be tiring, to be alive is to be dying. Opposites are bound together.

To illustrate his ideas Heraclitus used the example of a road on a hill. Is it going up or down? Well, it's neither one nor the other – it's both. The road is in a contradictory state. A road that goes up is also one that goes down. Similarly, the beginning of a circle is also its end. Everything is like this, existing by connection to its opposite. As Heraclitus wrote, 'We step into and we do not step into the same rivers. We are and we are not.'

This is why Heraclitus claimed that the universe is essentially made of fire, for it burns with the creative and destructive power of raging heat. Existence is an endless war, endless destruction, perpetual incineration. Every state is conquered by its opposite: youth by age, wakefulness by sleep, life by death. The universe is forever burning itself up and forever forging itself anew. Amid this upheaval there is only one changeless thing – change itself.

3

Zeno of Elea

Φ *Pronunciation* Zee-no
Φ *Time* 495-430 BCE
Φ *Born* Elea (Italy)
Φ *Quote* 'Not easily exhausted is the great strength of double-tongued Zeno, censurer of all,' Timon of Phlius.

Zeno of Elea could spit and think with equal ferocity. He was a tenacious individual who doggedly fought for truth and justice. No matter how hopeless his predicament, surrender was never an option. Philosophically, this meant defending the outlandish view that motion is an illusion (nothing *really* moves, the world is essentially still). Politically, it meant going to extreme and gruesome lengths (the aforementioned spitting, more on that later) to rid Elea, his hometown, of the tyrant Nearchus.

Zeno felt a deep connection to Elea. Though it was a small and insular town he was happy there. He didn't flounce off to the mountains like Heraclitus or crave the dynamism of Athens like Aristippus. He had everything he wanted in Elea, not least his boyfriend Parmenides, who was also a brilliant philosopher.

Though Elea couldn't boast the extensive philosophical community of Athens, Zeno and Parmenides were sufficiently stimulated by each other's company that they didn't need lively dinner parties or clamorous debates. Possibly to prove that they alone possessed more philosophical energy than the whole of Athens combined, one summer during the festival of Panathenaea (a celebration of the goddess Athena's birthday – 'birth' here is meant rather loosely given that Athena entered the world from the side of Zeus's head), Zeno and Parmenides visited the city to bewilder the Athenians with their theories and arguments.

Zeno knew that the theories he and Parmenides had been developing were likely to be rejected, even mocked. But he wasn't intimidated, he relished the fight. He was the first philosopher to see philosophy as a battle, believing that the philosopher's job is to pulverise and crush one's intellectual enemies with compelling arguments. And so he arrived in Athens ready and armed, carrying with him a book that contained forty explosive arguments.

With the book in hand Zeno stood beneath the sultry sun and declaimed his arguments. A few passers-by stopped, most of whom (Socrates included) simply wanted to marvel at his strikingly handsome face and impressive stature. Within moments, however, these unsuspecting Athenians were struck with befuddlement. Stupefied, they listened while Zeno carefully peeled away the reality of motion, methodically explaining why it must be the case that there is no movement in the universe.

Though this may sound like whimsy, Zeno was entirely serious. If he were asked why the chicken crossed the road, he would have retorted in earnest that it didn't, it couldn't! And this, to get to the philosophical heart of the matter, is because in order to cross the road the chicken would be required to perform an infinite amount of tasks in a finite time, which is manifestly impossible.

To start with, imagine that the chicken wanted to perform the less daring task of crossing a small 12cm wide puddle. Let's call the near edge A and the far edge B. To cross from A to B the chicken would need to first cover half the distance, crossing the interval from A to A_α.

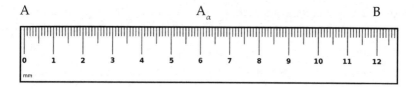

So the task of crossing from A to B actually involves two tasks: crossing from A to A_α and then A_α to B. But this isn't all. To move from A to A_α the chicken would need to first reach the midpoint between these, A_β.

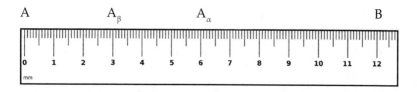

We now realise that the task of crossing from A to B actually involves three tasks: crossing the interval from A to A_β, and then from A_β to A_α, and finally from A_α to B.

But the chicken's tasks don't end here. To cross from A to A_β, the chicken would need to cross half *that* distance:

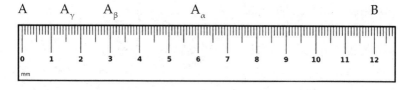

Yet to travel from A to A_γ, the chicken would again need to cover half of that distance. Can you see where this is going? Well, in fact, nowhere at all. This need to cross to the halfway point is without end: to travel 12cm the chicken first needs to travel 6cm, but to travel 6cm it first needs to travel 3cm, and to travel 3cm it first needs to travel 1.5cm, and to travel 1.5cm it first needs to travel 0.75cm, and so on, forever.

Zeno therefore argued that to travel from A to B requires

performing an infinite number of tasks, but since it's impossible to achieve this in a finite time, it's therefore impossible for the chicken to reach B. This is not only true for the chicken, it's the case for all of us whenever we endeavour to splash through a puddle, or cross a road, or fly over an ocean, or traverse any distance whatsoever. Every distance contains an infinite number of tasks that we must perform, which we never can, and therefore motion is an illusion.

The Athenians were incredulous. One philosopher, a Cynic called Antisthenes, grew impatient and yelled, 'No such thing as motion? Let me prove you wrong, Zeno,' and stormed off.

This didn't deter Zeno. He certainly understood that there *appears* to be motion in the universe. Yet he also understood that appearances can be deceiving. He believed that we ought to trust logic and reason rather than our senses to tell us what the world is really like.

Zeno continued with another argument. He asked his audience to consider one of the alleged features of motion: the apparent fact that some objects move faster than others and are thereby able to overtake them.

Think of Achilles, the hero of the Trojan War famous for his startling speed. Imagine he were racing against a plodding tortoise whom he allowed a 50m head start. It wouldn't take very long for Achilles to overtake the tortoise, right? Wrong! According to Zeno, Achilles can never overtake the tortoise.

Why? Well, to start with it seems obviously true that to overtake someone who is ahead of you, you first need to reach the point they're currently occupying. However, if they're not stationary, by the time you reach the point they *were* occupying, they are no longer there and have moved on to a new point. Yet by the time you reach that new point, they've moved on again to yet another point, and by the time you reach that point, they've moved on... and so on. You can never actually reach them.

In the case of Achilles and the tortoise, if the tortoise is currently at x, to overtake the tortoise Achilles will have to reach x. However, by the time Achilles has reached this point, the tortoise has moved forward slightly to y. Again, Achilles cannot overtake him without now first reaching y. However, once again, by the time Achilles has reached this point, the tortoise has progressed slightly to z. And so every time Achilles reaches the point where the tortoise has just been, the tortoise has moved on slightly. And so Achilles will never catch up with or overtake the tortoise.

Zeno argued that this proves that one of the essential features of motion (the ability of faster objects to catch up with and overtake slower ones) is impossible, and therefore motion itself is impossible.

The crowd were no more receptive to this argument than the first. An archer who was on his way to the Panathenaea games attempted his own version of Antisthenes' proof by drawing an arrow out of his quiver and firing it high towards the sun.

'Zeno, are you blind? Did you not see the arrow flying towards the sun?' he asked.

Zeno wasn't troubled by this demonstration. 'Can an object be in two different places at the same time?' he asked.

'Certainly not,' the archer replied.

'And if an object cannot be in two different places at the same time, it follows that at any given instant in time, an object can only occupy one place, correct?'

'Yes.'

'Yet an object that only occupies one place is stationary, is it not?'

'Of course.'

'Therefore, at every instant during the arrow's flight it is stationary. And since its time in flight is made up of these instants, it follows that arrow is stationary throughout its flight.'

A few in the audience laughed at this, convinced by now that Zeno was some sort of comedian. Others were agitated rather than amused. But there were a few who were deeply and intellectually troubled by these arguments. Indeed, Zeno's arguments do seem to make sense, yet their conclusions are also seemingly absurd. A crazy conclusion which follows from good reasoning is known as a paradox. To this day philosophers still think about and try to solve Zeno's paradoxes.

Returning to that afternoon in the 5th century BCE, since the archer didn't know how to defeat Zeno's logic he resorted to threats and intimidation.

'Go back to Elea,' he growled. 'Leave this place, leave Athens. Go!'

'Happily, happily,' Zeno replied. 'Though before I do, I feel it my duty to inform you that there is in fact no such thing as place. Give me a mo, I've developed this argument – now where is it? Ah yes,' said Zeno, tapping a page in his book.

'Everything exists in a place, which means that if *place* exists it must itself have a place, but then that place must have a place, and this would go on to infinity, which doesn't make sense. Therefore, nothing has a location, and therefore, strictly speaking I cannot leave this place since it doesn't exist, you see?'

Zeno looked up to find the archer aiming an arrow squarely at his forehead. Despite the fabulous time he was having, he sensed it was time to go home.

Clearly, Zeno was a plucky and pugnacious philosopher who was willing to defend the apparently indefensible despite ridicule and opposition. These same qualities would become grotesquely apparent years later when Elea was at the mercy of the despicable ruler Nearchus.

With a group of fellow Eleatics Zeno led a plot to overthrow the tyrant, but his plan was foiled and the philosopher was thrown in jail. During his interrogation he was ordered to reveal the names of his co-conspirators, but he lied, cleverly telling Nearchus that the people involved were the tyrant's own friends. Outraged, Nearchus swiftly had them executed, and was thereby left with fewer allies.

When the deception was discovered he had Zeno bound to a tree in the centre of the town to be tortured. He declared to the townspeople, who had been rounded up to watch the horror, that Zeno's torture would only end once he revealed the names of the other conspirators – and then it would be their turn.

After a period of excruciating pain Zeno said that he was ready to offer the names. With a weary voice he asked Nearchus to lean in so he could whisper them to him. Once the tyrant was within range, Zeno lunged forwards and bit down hard on his ear, tearing it clean off the side of his head. Nearchus screamed in agony as blood sprayed out of the wound. Boiling with rage, he drew a dagger and held it to Zeno's hairline. 'You will tell me the names or I will carve off your face and feed it to my dogs,' he said.

Zeno wasn't cowed. He looked at the townspeople, most of whom were watching through their fingers. 'Cowards!' he cried out. 'Cowards, all of you! Do you not see that Nearchus's power consists of nothing but your own fear?'

He turned to Nearchus. 'Do as you wish, I will not speak,' and with that he stuck his tongue out between his teeth and snapped his jaws firmly shut, summoning all the force that he could muster to gnaw through the flesh. With the tongue fully severed he spat it out in Nearchus's face.

Emboldened by this bloody act of courage, the crowd rose up and stoned Nearchus to death. Elea was finally free of its oppressor.

4

Empedocles

Φ *Pronunciation* Em-ped-o-kleez
Φ *Time* 490-381 BCE
Φ *Born* Acragas (Sicily)
Φ *Quote* 'Under love we unite into a single ordered whole, which under strife again becomes, instead of one, many.'

There are at least two reasons why a person might choose to jump into a volcano. One: because they wish to die. Two: because they wish to prove that they can't die. For Empedocles it was the latter reason.

At the staggering, stooping age of 109 years old he felt that the time had finally come to show the world that he was no mere mortal. He believed that he was a god – a degree of self-confidence perhaps only available to champion athletes, which he'd been in his

youth – and he was hell-bent on proving it.

Thousands of supporters gathered on Mount Etna to watch this act of daring, or stupidity, or daring stupidity, or stupid daring – regardless, most were confident that he would emerge triumphant and uncooked. They had followed him for years and witnessed his astonishing acts. They had seen him bring the dead back to life, foretell the future, control the wind and rain. Surely, he was more than human...

Empedocles stood at the edge of the crater dressed in his typical purple robe, bronze shoes and crown. Though he could smell the molten heat singing the ends of his long hair, he felt no fear. He turned to the crowd and waved. Enthusiastically, they cheered and whooped, and then he was gone.

A hush descended over the spectators as they waited. After a few anxious moments they noticed something hurtling out of the crater.

'Look,' one of his followers cried. 'He has survived! And he has attained the power of flight! He truly is a god! All hail Empedocles!'

'Are you sure that's him? He looks rather... small,' another said.

The object flew directly over them, crashing several metres away. The crowd hurried over and to their amazement discovered that it was Empedocles – well, sort of, it was his foot.

There, melting in the gravel, was one of his bronze shoes, and there inside it was his charred foot.

'Where's the rest of him?' someone asked.

'I think that's all that's left,' another replied.

'So I guess...'

'... he wasn't a god.'

'So I guess...'

'... he was just a man.'

'So I guess...'

'... he's dead.'

They stared at each other wondering what to do now.

'Maybe he'll be reincarnated!' one suddenly exclaimed.

A ripple of excitement spread through the crowd.

'Look!' another cried, pointing to a butterfly that went flitting by. 'It is Empedocles returned to us!'

A cheer erupted and off they went chasing the butterfly

down the mountain.

This belief in reincarnation was no mere coincidence with the ideas of chapter 1. Though Empedocles's followers learnt these ideas from him, he had learnt them from the Pythagoreans. For a brief period he had been a member of the commune, but he was excommunicated for revealing the teachings of Pythagoras to outsiders. As someone who was suspicious of authority – he had himself declined kingship – Empedocles found it difficult to follow rules.

Like Pythagoras, Empedocles was able to remember his former lives. He could recall being men, women, birds, even bushes. And like Pythagoras he believed that eating meat was cannibalism (he also shared his teacher's curious bean phobia). To eat a cow is not only to eat a creature that we once were, or may have been, it is also to eat a creature with which we share a basic kinship since we are all essentially wandering souls in temporary bodies.

Despite the similarities with his erstwhile teacher, Empedocles had his own original and wildly inventive ideas about the universe. He believed that there are two basic forces controlling everything: love and strife. Love is a force that unifies and ties everything together whereas strife tears it all apart. These two forces take turns in domination. The universe is either in a process of ever tightening unity or ever loosening fragmentation. Everything is either coming together or falling to pieces.

Once love has exerted its full influence the universe merges into a single cosmic sphere (a state not dissimilar to how scientists today conceive of the universe prior to the Big Bang). Within this sphere there are no longer individual beings or objects. The boundaries and borders of things melt away.

This unifying process is also responsible for our friendships and attractions. Love is not a human peculiarity. It acts on all things, from clouds to comets to kittens. The same force that binds atoms and molecules together also generates our bonds of longing and compassion.

When total harmony has been achieved and there is nothing left to unify, strife gets to work. It descends over the universe as a vortex, ripping the elements apart. The cosmic sphere is torn to pieces; the one thing becomes many things. This splintering force is the same power that generates human hatred, conflict, division and war. And it works both across and within us: eventually the human body will disintegrate, its pieces sundered, our DNA unravelled.

This alternating cycle of love and strife is endless. When the shreds of existence are at maximum disorder and strife can cause no further fragmentation, love returns. Bodies start to reassemble. The world crawls with lonely limbs seeking other body parts in the hope of forming complete organisms. This happens chaotically, without design or purpose, and from out of this lottery hideous combinations take shape: faces full of ears, frogs covered in fingers, human-headed lions.

These monstrosities are unable to live for long. Only those creatures whose combined parts ensure their survival are able to continue and reproduce (a process not dissimilar to what scientists today call natural selection). Human existence, therefore, is a matter of luck, and of love, though the love is temporary, and our existence will not pass peaceably but end amid the mincing, grinding blizzards of strife.

5

Buddha

Φ *Pronunciation* Bood-ah
Φ *Time* 484-404 BCE
Φ *Born* Kapilavastu (Nepal)
Φ *Theory* Buddhism

Misery and suffering. Does it ever seem to you that there is little else? Do you ever wonder why the world is consumed by bitterness and anger? Are you plagued by the feeling that life is essentially without purpose? Do you long to escape this endless parade of dissatisfaction, jealousy, and fear? The Buddha certainly did. These were the worries that exercised and befuddled him. They were the questions he sought to answer.

Ordinarily and often we are involved in the struggle to end particular instances of suffering, perhaps through a consoling conversation with a friend to repair a broken heart, or devouring a tub of ice cream to compensate for a disappointment. Extraordinarily, however, the Buddha wanted to end *all* suffering, to eliminate suffering itself, and not with everlasting cuddles or endless ice cream, but with knowledge of what suffering truly is. He wanted to unearth what lay at the root of our pain and anguish, and this led him to ask a remarkable question: *Do we expect too much of the world?*

Certainly, it came as no surprise to those who were present at the Buddha's (whose name was Siddhartha Gautama, 'Buddha' is a title meaning enlightened one) birth that he grew up to lead an extraordinary life. After emerging out of his mother's side the newborn child immediately took seven steps and proclaimed, 'I am chief of the world.' Evidently, he was rather special.

The Buddha's father, however, did not want a special son,

at least not one who devoted his life to exploring the mysteries of existence and suffering. He wanted a son who would grow to become powerful and rich, just as he was. So when a seer foretold that there were two possible futures for the Buddha, one in which he would become a wealthy political ruler like his father and another in which he would renounce his privilege to discover profound truths, his father did everything within his power to annihilate the latter possibility.

If the Buddha was likely to renounce his status in order to seek an end to suffering, the Buddha's father reasoned that the best way to prevent this was to ensure that the Buddha neither experienced nor witnessed any suffering. And so he went to great expense to ensure that his son's every wish was satisfied, that their palace was only staffed with young and beautiful employees, and that the Buddha lived healthily and never fell victim to illness. And the plan, this great deception, was a success, but only for a time.

For 29 years the Buddha lived a life insulated from hardship and pain. Guarded by the wide walls of his palace the Buddha believed that life was an eternal holiday, an unbroken stream of carefree days. There he lived with his wife and son in a state of perfect harmony. It was a life of pure happiness, but it was built on lies, and the harsh realities of existence could not be hidden forever.

One day when the Buddha took a chariot ride beyond the palace walls he observed three distressing sights: an elderly person, a sick person and a corpse. He asked the charioteer why some people suffer from these afflictions. The charioteer gently informed him that these are universal afflictions suffered by us all and that no one is immune to the processes of aging, illness and death.

Though for us these facts are obvious and ordinary, due to the Buddha's insulated upbringing he saw them with fresh and startled eyes. The revelation was an earthquake. Everything that once seemed fixed and solid now appeared desperately fragile and ultimately doomed. He was filled with despair.

'If everything eventually becomes nothing, then ultimately there is no purpose to anything,' he thought to himself.

At the palace that evening he tried to distract himself from these thoughts. He reclined

on a bed of cushions and ordered a troop of dancers to perform for him, but he couldn't forget what he had seen. When he looked at the athletic bodies of the dancers he saw only the gyrations of rotting corpses. His perception of the present was haunted by the knowledge of its inevitable decay.

Amid the Buddha's gloom, however, there was one slender ray of hope. That day he had not only seen the old, the sick and the dead, he had also seen a holy mendicant, a religious man who supported himself through begging. Despite the suffering everywhere around him, he walked through the world with a serene smile. Had he discovered the solution to the problem of suffering? The Buddha was encouraged by the possibility and he resolved to leave his life of wealth and pleasure in order to find this solution.

Later that night he crept into his son's bedroom to hold him for the last time but was saddened to find that he had fallen asleep in his wife's arms: if he took the boy, she would surely wake and try to stop him. And so, without a final embrace, the Buddha left the palace and disappeared into the night.

The next morning, as he knelt beside a river he noticed in the reflection his fine silken clothes and long lustrous hair. These were signs of his former life and they had to be discarded. By remaining attached to the life of pleasure he would not find the solution to suffering. And so he tossed away his clothes and cut his hair with a sword.

Those who encountered him had no notion of his former wealth and standing. As he travelled from door to door begging for alms he was seen as just another mendicant. Despite his humble appearance he initially found it difficult to adapt to the poverty of this new life, particularly the food. The meals he was offered were revolting and made him want to throw up. This wasn't so much a judgment as a physiological reaction. His body wasn't accustomed to foods so devoid of pleasure. With discipline, however, he learnt to overcome his disgust and tolerate the gruel.

His capacity for self-discipline soon received a far greater test when he encountered a group of five men who were similarly attempting to overcome suffering. Their method involved practices of extreme self-denial: eating one grain of rice a day and reducing their breath in order to deprive their bodies of oxygen. It was as though they were attempting to overcome suffering by proving that they were stronger than it. If they could survive extreme states of self-induced hunger, weakness and fatigue without submitting to their appetites and needs, they would thereby prove themselves superior to those needs. The Buddha was inspired by this group of ascetics and decided to follow their lead. Like them he ate only one grain of rice per day and performed breath-suppressing exercises.

After six years of living this way he was skeletal. His skin had lost its golden glow and was so tight to the bone that his eye sockets were visible. His hair was falling out and he was so weak he could only stand with great difficulty. The lack of oxygen from the breathing techniques left him with constant, excruciating headaches.

He realised that this was not the solution to the problem of suffering. The solution was not to be found in a show of strength or superiority. He didn't want to prove his superiority to suffering but to achieve liberation from it. He wanted freedom, not victory. And so he abandoned this self-denying life.

The five men were dismayed to see the Buddha eat his first full meal for six years. They believed that his years of effort and hard work had been undone in a matter of minutes. But the Buddha didn't see things this way. He believed that he had gained a valuable insight: neither his life of indulgence nor his life of denial brought an end to suffering. The solution, he realised, was not to be found in states of extremity but in a life of balance.

After regaining his strength the Buddha sat beneath a fig tree on the banks of the Nairanjana River one evening, closed his eyes and resolved not to move till he had once and for all found the solution to suffering. While he sat simply focusing on his breathing – not trying to control it as he had done before – he noticed that various feelings arose in him, such as fear, doubt, hunger and thirst. But he didn't recoil from these feelings, nor did he try to suppress them, he simply noticed them, and soon they passed. It was during this state of cool detachment that the Buddha felt great waves of serenity and joy suddenly wash over him. And it was then he realised that he had finally freed himself from suffering.

Whereas the group of five ascetics were trying to do battle with suffering, the Buddha now understood that any attempt to overcome suffering without knowledge of its true nature was hopeless. And this is what he now possessed: understanding, or enlightenment. Sitting beneath the tree, allowing his mind to wander and drift, he realised that attachment was the cause of suffering.

Recall the earlier question: *Do we expect too much of the world?* The Buddha's answer was a resounding yes. We expect permanence and stability, but this is hopeless for nothing is permanent or stable, nothing lasts. The world and our desires are always shifting, and so we are never satisfied. We crave wealth, but no sooner have we acquired it than we crave more. We crave the unity of true love, but our partner changes, or we change, and the feeling of oneness falls to pieces. We crave admiration for our accomplishments, but once those accomplishments fade into the past, the admiration we received fades with them.

The longing to hold onto and possess fragments of a fleeting world leads to crushing disappointment, thereby sowing the seeds for feelings of sadness, greed and anger. Remember the three sights that plunged the Buddha into such despair. He now realised that by being unattached to youth, health and life, he would no longer suffer from their inevitable passing. Freedom from attachment and craving is freedom from suffering.

An essential requirement in attaining this freedom is letting go of our attachment to ourselves and ideas of our own identity. There are no essences in a forever changing world, and since this is a world we are a part of, there is no essence to us. Beneath our fleeting thoughts, shifting moods and changing bodies there is no permanent self. We should not seek to define ourselves or unearth the truth of who we really are. It is as hopeless as raking leaves in a storm.

Understanding this joyful hopelessness liberates us from the pains of greed and jealousy. If we have no self, there is no use in trying to fabricate one out of ever-growing wealth or possessions. And having no self, there is no sense in measuring ourselves against others. Happily, we are able to abandon the frantic quest to be something, or somebody. And with this we are likewise freed of the burdens of remorse and guilt. Since our past actions do not define us, our prior wrongs need not haunt us. Unshackled from the self-absorption of our own guilt, unencumbered by the longing for identity, we can move through the world selflessly and generously.

For seven weeks the Buddha sat beneath the tree enjoying the bliss of his liberation from suffering. Eventually, however, he decided to share these insights with others, to help awaken those who remained asleep to the truth of suffering. His first students were the five ascetics. He walked 150 miles to offer them all he had learnt, and after this first sermon he continued to teach for 45 years.

Of course, a vital part of his teaching was that his students should not become attached to his teaching. Attachment to ideas is just as troublesome as the attachment to feelings or belongings. What we mustn't do is *crave* an end to suffering. We can only become enlightened once we no longer seek enlightenment.

The Buddha's students were often frustrated with him. Not only did he instruct them to take to heart the seemingly paradoxical teaching that they should not take his teachings to heart, he also declined to answer many of their questions. When he was asked whether the self exists, or whether the universe is infinite, or whether the body and soul are identical, he would remain silent. Though he didn't believe in a lasting self, he didn't want his students to become attached to the idea of its non-existence. The aim is not to form a belief that the self does not exist but to liberate ourselves from the very idea of a self. To even speculate about its existence shows an unhealthy attachment to the idea.

After many decades of wandering and teaching the Buddha was old and tired. By the age of 80 his frail body was like an old faltering cart precariously held together with threads of string. And so he decided it was time to die. For his final meal he requested a dish called pig's delight (whether this dish was one that pigs delight in, like truffles, or one that consisted of delighting in pigs, like bacon, no one quite knows) which unfortunately caused him a terrible bout of dysentery. He then lay down beneath two trees which, as a result of his presence, blossomed out of season. Moments later, with the silence of falling snow, he gave up his life force and died.

Like Pythagoras and Empedocles, the Buddha believed in reincarnation. However, he also believed that those who had achieved enlightenment were thereby freed from the endless cycle of rebirth. And so this life was the Buddha's last.

You may well wonder whether the enlightened continue to exist after death. Certainly, the Buddha was often asked this question. But he never answered.

6

Socrates

Φ *Pronunciation* Sock-ra-teez
Φ *Time* 469-399 BCE
Φ *Born* Athens (Greece)
Φ *Quote* 'The unexamined life is not worth living.'

Socrates is famous for being dead. Or rather, he's famous for the manner in which he died. To cut a long story short, he annoyed his fellow Athenians to such a degree that they executed him. But then they realised that they missed him and so erected a statue in his honour. And today he is regarded as one of the most important philosophers who ever lived.

None of this would have come to pass had it not been for a tiny voice in Socrates' head. He was a formidable soldier (he fought against Sparta in the Peloponnesian Wars) and a skilled speaker, and he could have led a successful and comfortable life in Athens. Wealth and luxury were within his reach, but he shunned them. Turning away from public life he instead chose philosophy, poverty and pillory. And it was the tiny voice that made him do it.

Ever since he was a child Socrates was able to hear this spirit voice talking to him, guiding him. But it would only proscribe and never prescribe, it didn't tell him what to do, only what *not* to do. Having told him *not* to devote his time and energy to the politics of Athens, his life was a vacuum of possibilities. It was not until the intervention of another supernatural being, Apollo (god of light), that his life found a clear purpose.

As was common among the Greeks, a friend of Socrates one day embarked on a journey of many miles to visit the Delphic oracle, a woman through whom the god Apollo offered advice and prophesy. One of the questions he asked the oracle was this: 'Is any person wiser than Socrates?' To his friend's astonishment the oracle replied, 'There is no person wiser than Socrates.'

The man rushed back to Athens to tell Socrates what he had heard. This befuddled Socrates greatly. 'How can I be the wisest? I don't know anything,' he mused.

Socrates decided to test the oracle's pronouncement by finding and conversing with those people who were thought to be wise. He spoke to politicians, but it didn't take long before he realised that they were in fact fools. He then spoke to poets, who were similarly stupid. To Socrates' surprise he discovered that if you investigate a person's beliefs by asking them a few probing questions, you quickly realise that they don't actually know what they think about anything.

Most people didn't appreciate Socrates exposing them in this way and were exasperated by his questioning. A typical conversation with a politician might proceed as follows:

'What is your role?'

'To govern the city.'

'What is a city?'

'It is the roads and buildings we see around us.'

'So you are here to govern roads and buildings?'

'No, I am here to govern the people of the city.'

'So are you here to govern the people or the city?'

'The people.'

'You said the city to start with.'

'I meant the people.'

'So you do not govern Athens?'

'Of course I do!'

'Is Athens a city?'

'Yes, the greatest.'

'Yet, you just said you do not govern the city.'

'I meant that – um – I said that… Now see here, is this some kind of trick? Who do you think you are? Get lost, you ugly freak!' (With his bulging eyes, snub nose and pot belly, it was not uncommon for Socrates to be called ugly.)

The politicians who were meant to govern the city didn't even  know what a city was. But they were far from exceptional in their ignorance. Socrates realised that *everyone* was clueless. There was not a single person who could precisely explain the meaning of their dearly held beliefs. He thus understood why the Delphic oracle had called him the wisest person: he was the wisest precisely because he knew he wasn't wise. Everyone else was too stupid to realise how stupid they were. But he, Socrates, knew he was stupid, and that made him the least stupid of all.

He now saw it as his duty to make the Athenians realise their stupidity. This is what the god wanted of him. He believed that ignorance is incompatible with a good life since we are only able to lead a good life if we know what goodness is. And we can only begin to investigate the nature of goodness once we have realised that we don't understand its nature. Therefore, the quest for a good life must start with a frank acceptance of our own cluelessness, just as the quest for good governance must start with a politician's admission that they don't know what a city is.

Unlike Heraclitus who grew so frustrated with everyone else's stupidity that he lived alone in the mountains, Socrates took it upon himself to discuss philosophy with all who would engage with him. He spent his days wandering through the marketplace challenging people to explain their beliefs. Naturally, he received a lot of abuse. He'd stop someone who was buying, say, olives and ask, 'What is the greatest virtue?'

'Courage is the greatest virtue,' they might reply.

'And what is courage?'

'Fearlessness.'

'Does a lion who hunts a mouse have fear?'

'Of course not. A lion has nothing to fear from a mouse.'

'Is the lion courageous for hunting a mouse?'

'Not in the slightest.'

'But the lion is fearless, and you said that courage was fearlessness.'

'No, I meant... fearlessness when there is something to fear.'

'By that definition a drunkard who stumbles into a zoo enclosure to pet the lions must be courageous.'

'No, they are foolish!'

'But they are being fearless in the face of something fearful, so according to you they must be courageous.'

'No, I didn't mean – um – I meant...'

'How can you claim to admire courage when you don't even know what it is?'

Comments such as this would inevitably be followed by a fist in Socrates' ugly face. But he didn't mind. He would get back up, dust himself down and find someone else to question. He understood that befuddlement can be unpleasant.

The reaction to Socrates was not only one of hostility. Some Athenians, mostly the children of the rich, admired the way he was able expose the stupidity of their pompous elders. At first his followers tried to pay him, but he refused their money. Some of them, wishing to express their gratitude, insisted: 'Socrates, with this money you could dine at the finest restaurants and eat the finest food.' But he would reply: 'Others live to eat, I simply eat to live. I have no need for your money.'

It should be stressed, however, that Socrates was not their teacher, for the obvious reason that he had nothing to teach, no knowledge to impart. Philosophy for him was an investigation, a process of discovery, a quest. The philosopher trades in questions, not answers.

Nevertheless, Socrates did at times express his own views. For instance, he thought that no one ever intentionally acts badly: we always do what we *think* is right, even if it is actually wrong. As such, he believed that for people to become good they only needed to learn what goodness was. Once we know it, we'll follow it. This is a vital endeavour because it is impossible for a bad person to have a happy life.

Despite his tendency to annoy his fellow citizens Socrates managed to live a long life. It wasn't till he was 70 years old that several Athenians decided enough was enough and had him put on trial. Socrates' friends begged him to flee the city, but his inner voice, that guiding spirit, was silent on the matter, indicating that there was no good reason to avoid the trial. And so before a jury of 501 he was charged with impiety and corrupting the young.

There were no professional lawyers in Athens, so Socrates defended himself before the court. 'It is foolish to call me impious when I consider myself the god's gift to you,' he argued.

'By encouraging you to think about goodness and how we ought to live, I have done this city the greatest possible service. If anything, I do not deserve punishment but gratitude. My personal view is that a lifetime of free dinners would be a suitable reward, but as things stand, I would settle for not being executed.

'With respect to the charge of corrupting the young, how is this possible when I have never taught them a single thing?

How am I capable of polluting their minds when I do not even know what I think?'

Alas, his arguments failed to persuade the jury who, by a margin of 30 votes, sentenced him to death. He spent his final month in prison awaiting execution. His friends begged him to escape and flee Athens, but he refused. He argued that we should respect the laws of our cities as we do the rules of our parents. The city *is* our parent. It has raised and nurtured us. To violate the law by running away would be akin to slapping one's mother or father in the face. And so he stayed in his cell, spending his days dancing in his chains or conversing with his friends.

On the day of his execution he said farewell to his wife and children. He told his friends to stop snivelling and calmly downed the poison (hemlock). Lying on his bed, he waited for the rising numbness to paralyse his beating heart.

Shortly after his death the Athenians felt a cloud of sadness descend over the city. There was an undeniable sense of emptiness. Could it be... were they pining for Socrates? Did they actually miss him? It was true! They *were* pining, they *did* miss him. They missed scuttling away whenever they saw his grotesque face in this distance. They missed his infuriating questions.

Regretting his death, the Athenians tried to make amends by banishing or executing his original accusers. They then built a bronze statue in his likeness. It was all that could be done to fill the Socrates-shaped hole that had been left in the city.

7

Aristippus

Φ *Pronunciation* A-wrist-i-puss
Φ *Time* 435-356 BCE
Φ *Born* Cyrene (Libya)
Φ *Theory* Hedonism

Not all philosophers are befuddled by life. Not all wonder what it is or what its purpose might be. Consider Aristippus. He was never befuddled by life's meaning. Why? Because he didn't believe life could have a meaning. And he didn't believe life could have a meaning because he didn't believe there was any such thing as life!

What on earth did Aristippus mean by this? Did he believe that we are all in fact dead?

Well no, he didn't think that. He certainly believed in the existence of living things. He just didn't believe in *life*. That is to say, while it's true that we are alive, it's not true that we *have* a life. And the reason we don't have a life is because the present moment is all that exists. Unlike the present, the past and future aren't real. Questions such as, 'How has my life changed since last year?' or 'Where is my life heading?' don't actually make sense. Our existence is a vanishing staircase. There is no yesterday or tomorrow. This moment right now is all that we have.

Rather than trying to achieve a happy life, Aristippus believed we should only seek a pleasurable present. Whereas happiness is an ongoing psychological state, pleasure is an immediate experience which can be parcelled into the smallest moments; cakes and jokes and naps can bring us pleasure, though not necessarily happiness. Aristippus believed that pleasure was the only and ultimate good thing in the world: everything that causes pleasure is good and everything that causes pain is bad.

Though these ideas were radically different to Socrates', Aristippus was at one time a student of the Athenian. In fact, growing up in North Africa he was positively ensorcelled by the stories he heard of Socrates wandering the streets of Athens accosting the locals with befuddling questions while asserting that the highest wisdom is the realisation that we have none.

Aristippus experienced such a longing to learn from Socrates that he suffered a physical breakdown and became dangerously thin. The only solution was to venture across the Mediterranean Sea to meet his hero, which is precisely what he did. And though Aristippus was certainly not disappointed by the philosopher he found, once he had absorbed everything that Socrates had to offer, he separated from him and started to instruct his own pupils in his own way.

The fact that Aristippus became a very different philosopher to Socrates is no indication of Socrates' failure. In philosophy it is common for one's followers to wander off in their own direction and discover their own thoughts. Trying to make two philosophers think in the same way is rather like trying to reproduce the exact same pattern by flicking a paintbrush twice. Nature just won't allow it.

One of the clearest and most immediate differences between these two philosophers was financial. Whereas Socrates insisted that he didn't want to be paid for his services, Aristippus would only teach those who could afford his considerable fees.

Puzzled by his riches Socrates asked him, 'What did you do to earn so much money?'

'Precisely what you do to earn so little,' he replied.

It may sound contradictory, but the reason Aristippus charged such high fees was because he didn't care about money. He wanted to loosen the attachment people felt towards money and to help them realise that money in itself has no value, its sole use is in helping us to acquire that which is truly valuable: pleasure.

This indifference to money enabled Aristippus to live lavishly. (Of course, he didn't save anything; there is no point saving for a future that doesn't exist.) When out for dinner he once spent the equivalent of £500 on a roasted partridge. When his dinner companion chided him for spending so much and being too attached to pleasure, he asked his companion whether he would have bought the same meal for £5. When his companion answered in the affirmative, Aristippus said, 'Well, to me £500 is worth no more than £5. The problem is not that I am attached to pleasure. It is that you are attached to money.'

Another time when his servant was carrying Aristippus's gold coins and finding the weight burdensome, Aristippus instructed him to pour them away till he could manage. The servant protested that this would be wasteful, and he laboured on.

'Do not be a fool,' Aristippus said. 'We earn money in order to lighten life's burdens, not add to them.'

A rich man who asked Aristippus to teach his son was appalled by the philosopher's price. 'For that sum I could buy a slave,' he objected.

'Then do so,' was Aristippus's reply, 'and you will have two.'

He believed that philosophy enables us to determine our own ideas about life and how we should live. A slave, on the other hand, is condemned to follow orders. And so, like a slave, someone not educated in philosophy will never become fully independent. They will never free themselves from mindless compliance. It is this capacity for free thought that distinguishes the life of the philosopher.

When Aristippus was caught in a storm at sea he reacted by squealing with panic and fear. One of the sailors was surprised by this and said, 'We ordinary folk are not alarmed, but you, a philosopher, weep like a coward.' Aristippus looked the man over and replied, 'Our lives are not equal: as a philosopher I have much more to lose.'

His life was more valuable because it was solely devoted to pleasure, which is all that matters. Those who expressed disapproval of his hedonism were merely voicing their own ignorance. They lived for pride, or honour, or meaning, or the future, but these are illusions. Young children in fact possess a greater understanding of life than adults. Children simply follow their appetites and desires, living from moment to moment with minds unclouded by the fictions of life.

Aristippus's most lucrative pupil was Dionysius I, the king of Syracuse in Sicily. The king wasn't only interested in matters of the mind. He also enjoyed silliness and games. On one occasion he stopped Aristippus and said, 'I must discuss an urgent matter with you.'

'What is it?' the philosopher asked.

The king replied by spitting in his face and walking away in a fit of laughter. Aristippus shrugged his shoulders and wiped his face.

A passer-by who saw the incident chided Aristippus for his lack of self-respect. Aristippus thought for a second before replying, 'Fishermen allow themselves to get soaked in seawater just to catch simple cod. Why should I not be wetted with slobber in order to fill my plate with fine caviar?'

He didn't care about what certain actions *meant* or what others thought of him. The soggy outcome of getting sprayed by water and getting spat on were essentially the same, so it makes no sense to be furious about the latter if we tolerate the former. Similarly, when asked whether he believed that his girlfriend truly loved him, he said he didn't care, just as he didn't care whether the wine he drank or the fish he ate loved him. While there is certainly sensual pleasure in being kissed, there is no sensual pleasure in being loved, and so the emotions behind the kisses were unimportant to him.

This disregard for the feelings of others did, however, lead him to behave in ways that most would regard as extremely cruel. When he left his baby son on a mountain to die of exposure he defended his actions by saying, 'Phlegm, too, is a product of the body, and we do not think it wrong to spit it away.'

One of the reasons why he was capable of acting so disreputably was because he refused to listen to those who criticised him. Once when he was being reproached for his extravagant way of life, he simply turned and walked away.

'Excuse me! Where are you going?' his critic asked.

'Just as it is your privilege to criticise me, it is my privilege not to listen.'

Fortunately, he did not treat all of his children with the callousness shown to his unwanted son. After he died his ideas continued to be taught by his daughter, Arete, whom he had trained in philosophy. She too became an esteemed and influential thinker and helped found a school known as the Cyrenaics, which was dedicated to her father's startling brand of hedonism.

8

Plato

Φ *Pronunciation* Play-toe
Φ *Time* 429-347 BCE
Φ *Born* Athens (Greece)
Φ *Theory* Platonism

Darkness is a deprivation. In the course of our nightly abandonment, after the sun has dipped below the horizon, we are deprived of the knowledge we formerly held of the world.

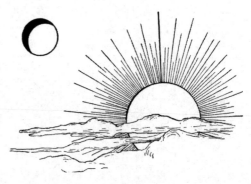

Amid the inky dark of a forest, a walker no longer knows what obstacles lie before her or what creatures may be behind her. She hears cracking twigs, but doesn't know the cause. She hears the cry of an animal, but doesn't know what it is or how close. The dark's deprivation is terrifying. Without knowledge of the world around her, she can only shuffle forwards, stumbling and floundering all the way.

Though these nightly trials are a passing affliction, Plato believed that for most of us this is our permanent state. Most of us live in a condition of unremitting darkness. Because we rely on our senses to understand the world we do not see and cannot know what it is really like. Our senses only reveal to us the outlines and shadows of reality. Your eyes only see what the sun is able to illuminate, but there is so much more to the world than can be touched by light. Those who rely entirely on their sensory experience to understand the world live amid the illusion of light, acquiring only the illusion of knowledge. To understand the world as it truly is, to escape the darkness, this cave of ignorance we are trapped in, we must strive to learn about the world using our minds alone.

Consider the property beauty. While there are many beautiful things in the world, you might think that none are purely and perfectly beautiful. Perfect beauty is never fully achieved. There is always something lacking. But to make this judgment, to recognise those manifold deficiencies, you must possess some understanding of perfect beauty.

Could this understanding have been attained through sensory observations? Seemingly not. Beauty does not possess size, shape or location. Since abstract properties are not physical, they lie beyond the perceptual reach of our physical bodies. So where does your understanding of beauty come from?

Plato concluded that this knowledge must have been acquired in a previous life, during an unearthly existence in which we possessed no body, no senses, and our intangible souls were acquainted with beauty itself. In this prior state we dwelt not among physical objects but abstract properties, the very essence of reality. With concerted thought and the efforts of philosophy we can recollect this lost knowledge. Those who try to understand beauty by studying beautiful things will fail. They will only attain the illusion of knowledge, see only the illusion of light. According to Plato beauty alone is purely and perfectly beautiful. The colours or sounds of beautiful things are mere copies and shadows of this purity and perfection. This is also true of many other properties, such as goodness and justice.

In the cases of justice and goodness Plato drew some startling conclusions. He believed that the only happy life was a good life, and since only those who know what goodness is are capable of attaining it, he reasoned that philosophers only (those who possessed knowledge and understanding) can be happy. The life of darkness within the gloomy cave of ignorance is ultimately unfulfilling. A full and happy life requires knowledge of the world as it truly is. It was for this reason that when he was asked to identify the world's most pleasant sound Plato replied, 'The truth.'

In addition to the claim that only philosophers can be happy, Plato argued that only philosophers should possess the power to rule over others. He claimed that only those who truly know what justice is are able to govern a just society. And only philosophers – those who have dedicated their lives to understanding reality – possess this knowledge.

Though Plato lived in a democratic society in which power was shared among the citizens of Athens (though not women and slaves), he despised this system of government. He believed that democracies only give the people what they want, not what they need. A good and just society will only arise once power has been withdrawn from the people and placed exclusively in the hands of those who know what's best: the philosopher-kings.

During his life Plato was afforded the opportunity to implement some of these ideas, but he failed miserably and emerged from the experiment lucky to be alive. Before looking at his blunders, let's rewind a little. Let's start with his name, which wasn't actually Plato but Aristocles. Plato was a nickname that derives from *platos*, meaning broad, which was possibly given to him in reference to his prodigious forehead.

Like many enemies of democracy, Plato, an Athenian native, was born into a rich and privileged family. It was thought that he could trace his ancestry back to the sea god Poseidon (the gods themselves, of course, were far from democratic in their governance of nature). He had at one time toyed with the idea of entering politics, but this was only one interest among many. He was also a wrestler, painter and poet. These numerous pursuits, however, were promptly cast aside the day he heard Socrates speak. From that day forth philosophy became his sole concern.

This pivotal moment occurred when Plato was 19 years old. He had been on his way to compete in a playwriting contest when he walked by Socrates philosophically interrogating a helpless victim. Plato was captivated by Socrates' thorough and unrelenting quest for truth, and so he threw his tragedy into a nearby fire and stayed to listen. Socrates then turned to Plato and gasped. 'You are the swan of my dream,' he said.

'You dreamt of me?' Plato asked, stunned.

'Last night I dreamt that a swan was standing on my knees. It spread out its brilliant white wings, emitted the sweetest of cries, and flew away. You are that swan, I recognise you.'

Thus began a rich and loving relationship, one that endured for nine years and ended only with Socrates' execution by the Athenians. Throughout that time Plato had shadowed him during his daily interrogations and he felt the loss of his master deeply.

Socrates' death put a decisive end to Plato's political ambitions: he could not participate in the governance of a city capable of such an injustice. Indeed, he couldn't even bear to live in the city any longer, and so he left. Like a moth in search of new light, Plato fled Athens and travelled to Libya, Egypt and Italy to learn from other philosophers.

When he was 40 years old Plato travelled to the city of Syracuse in Sicily where he met a young man named Dion who just was as enamoured of Plato as Plato had once been of Socrates. Dion listened keenly to Plato's teachings on the necessity of courage, moderation and wisdom for a happy life. Plato's ideas were in stark contrast to the lifestyles of the Sicilians whose main interests in life were sex and food. Dion was inspired by Plato's alternative and, in the pursuit of virtue and happiness, became an ardent student of philosophy. He felt that Plato's teachings might also prove hugely beneficial to his brother-in-law, the tyrant and ruler of Syracuse, Dionysius I.

Dionysius I was a murderous ruler who suffered from extreme paranoia. Fearful of being assassinated he wouldn't even permit his barber to cut his hair with scissors and instead had the ends singed with a hot coal. When one of his officers simply dreamt that he'd assassinated the tyrant, Dionysius I had him put to death, claiming that the dream revealed the officer's secret wish. The people of Syracuse lived in a state of constant anxiety.

Dion asked Plato whether he would meet with Dionysius I. Plato saw this as an opportunity to help mould a philosopher-king and agreed. But his encounter with Dionysius I was a disaster.

During a discussion on the nature of courage Plato made sure to emphasise that of all people tyrants such as Dionysius I possessed the least. He went on to explain that the lives of the just were far happier than the wretched lives of the unjust. Dionysius I was not accustomed to being spoken to in this manner and his fury was compounded by the admiration Plato received from the audience. The humiliated ruler abruptly ended the meeting and ordered for Plato to be placed on a boat, ostensibly to take him back to Greece, but with the secret order to either kill the philosopher or sell him into slavery.

Plato was deposited on the island of Aegina where the locals had a rule that the first Athenian to land on the island would be killed. As that first Athenian Plato's fate looked bleak, but he was eventually rescued by his friends who purchased his freedom and he soon returned to Athens.

Over the next two decades Plato ran his own school of philosophy outside the walls of Athens known as the Academy. There he would sit perched on a tree branch lecturing about the cave of darkness from which we must escape, and the changeless non-physical nature of reality of which the physical world of the senses is only a faint shadow.

In contrast to his prominent forehead, he was not an imposing character. He spoke softly and was fond of solitude. He rarely laughed. When Diogenes once interrupted his lecture swinging a plucked chicken and yelling that he had brought Plato another man to teach (this was a counter-example to Plato's admittedly flawed definition of humans as featherless bipeds), Plato didn't laugh, nor did he lose his temper. He simply waited for Diogenes to leave and continued without comment.

At some point during his 60s Plato's relationship with Syracuse was rekindled following a letter from Dion pleading him to return. By this time Dionysius I had died and his son Dionysius II was now the city's ruler. Dionysius II was scarcely an improvement over his father, but now the problem was excessive indifference, not excessive control. An infamous 90-day party in which he drank, danced and ignored his duties was illustrative of this neglect.

The problem was that the young man had not been readied for power. His father had refused to have his son educated for fear that he might use his learning to overthrow him. To both compensate for and exploit his lack of education, Dion believed that under Plato's tuition the young king could be shaped into a wise and just ruler of the kind Plato believed was necessary for a happy and stable society.

Plato was reluctant. He didn't want to be sold into slavery again! But if he didn't accede to Dion's plea he worried that he'd be called a coward and seen as someone who lacked the courage to put his ideas to the test. Since this might damage the reputation of philosophy he decided to return to Sicily.

Following the week-long journey Plato was welcomed by a magnificent royal chariot which collected him from the harbour. Within a matter of days Plato's influence was already evident. Dionysius II was acting with greater composure and self-possession. He was restraining his appetites by not indulging excessively in wine and food. But these changes alarmed Dionysius II's advisers who were unfamiliar with Plato's ideas about philosopher-kings. They feared that Dion's plan was for Plato to bewitch the ruler into stepping down, thereby allowing Dion to take his place.

Dionysius II was informed of these suspicions and promptly exiled Dion. He then placed Plato under house arrest and ordered his guards to keep a watchful eye on the philosopher. His lessons with Plato, however, didn't stop. Dionysius II continued to listen eagerly to Plato's ideas about the nature and importance of wisdom. He listened to the claims that the philosopher-kings should possess no private property and raise children communally so that their allegiance to the community is not compromised by their personal ties to family and possessions, but his ability to truly absorb these ideas was severely weakened by his growing infatuation with Plato.

The young ruler grew desperate for Plato's approval and became jealous of Plato's other friendships. This left him unable to bear criticism, which paralysed him philosophically;

too sensitive to hear Plato identify the flaws and errors in his ideas, he was unable to develop. Fortunately, this situation was resolved when Syracuse became embroiled in a war and Dionysius II permitted Plato to return to Athens.

A few years later Plato was persuaded to return to Sicily for his third and final time. Dionysius II wrote to Plato informing him that he longed for his tuition. The young king had been debating with other philosophers, trying to prove his philosophical superiority, without success; he wanted Plato to help guide him to victory. Plato was reluctant, but Dionysius II's jealousy of Dion had led him to block the exiled man from receiving the income he was owed from his properties in Sicily. He told Plato that if he returned Dion's income would be restored and his exile ended.

For this reason, as well as wanting to make a final attempt to create a philosopher-king, Plato ventured back across the sea. But once again he made little progress with Dionysius II and found himself living in grave danger in Syracuse. The hoodlums who were employed by the ruler to impose his regime of cruelty and violence on the people of Syracuse feared that they would lose their livelihoods if Plato succeeded in teaching Dionysius II to rule without tyranny, and so they plotted to have him killed.

Fortunately, Plato was granted permission to leave, and he resolved to never return. Since philosophy had failed to rid Syracuse of tyranny, Dion finally resorted to force. He assembled a small army and succeeded in overthrowing Dionysius II. But amid the consequent conflicts and power struggles he unfortunately had his throat slit.

In contrast to this turmoil Plato lived and taught amid the peace of his Academy for another decade. He died during his 80s, possibly from a severe lice infestation, and was allegedly buried in the grounds of the Academy, though to this day his grave has never been found.

9

Diogenes

Φ *Pronunciation* Die-odge-i-neez
Φ *Time* 404-323 BCE
Φ *Born* Sinope (Turkey)
Φ *Theory* Cynicism

Diogenes was an outsider, an oddball, he didn't fit in. It was the story of his life. He was an eternal loner.

Certainly, this saddened him, but only for a time. His sadness came to a decisive end the day he discovered something remarkable: life on the outside is far richer and more fulfilling than a life of acceptance and belonging. Having been rejected by society, Diogenes felt free to experiment with new ways of living, and the results were shocking, so much so that he became known as 'Socrates gone mad'.

He was originally from Sinope in Turkey but was forced to flee when the locals discovered that he had been replacing the gold in their coins with cheap metal. Arriving in Athens as a fugitive he wasn't warmly welcomed. None of the Athenians liked him. They resented how he criticised everything they said, and so he was never invited to dinner. Miserably, he would dine alone, eating bread and leaves for that was all he could afford.

One day a mouse came scurrying along to eat his crumbs. Instead of crushing the little beastie, Diogenes watched it at work, and he smiled, becoming more cheerful, and said, 'This mouse doesn't need luxuries or companionship, he doesn't need acceptance or admiration, and yet you, Diogenes, are upset at not dining with the Athenians.'

This thought comforted him greatly and he suddenly became befuddled as to why he had been so sad. Why had he sought acceptance if it meant trying to be something he wasn't? Why feel ashamed or embarrassed of our natural behaviour and instincts? Why not live with the freedom of mice? What sense is there in conforming to rules of good conduct when there are no compelling reasons for those rules?

Diogenes realised that his life would be vastly improved if he chose to live like an animal, following his natural inclinations, disregarding the expectations of society. Society is a den of fakes, a risible pantomime of phonies; a fact he would illustrate by walking the streets during the day while holding a lamp and saying that he was looking for a human being. Since there were no genuine human beings, no one who was true to their human nature, searching for one was as pointless an activity as using a flame to illuminate the day. In contrast to the fakes and conformists, Diogenes used reason to help him distinguish between what was natural and what was phoney, following the former while scorning the latter.

He became a distinctive sight on the streets of Athens, living in a sort of barrel and begging for money. He dressed shabbily and wore hardly any clothes, not caring whether his body was exposed. Ignoring the strictures of decency he would masturbate whenever and wherever he felt the need, commenting that he wished that he could likewise relieve his hunger simply by rubbing his belly.

Given the ineffectiveness of belly rubbing, like everyone else he sated his hunger with food. Unlike everyone else, however, he was happy to eat anything that he could find – dogs, rats, cats, anything – not worrying about whom it might belong to; he reasoned that since everything is ultimately owned by the gods, humans in fact own nothing, and so theft is a fiction. He would even eat human flesh, if there happened to be any lying around. To reiterate, he believed that reason helps us understand what is natural and what is mere convention, and thinking rationally, it was clear to Diogenes that human meat is essentially no different to the meat of a cow or a chicken, and so if it is permissible to eat one kind it must be permissible to eat all kinds. The Athenians were disgusted by his cannibalism, but this didn't bother Diogenes for their disgust was wholly unnatural.

His aim was to live without luxury, to strip life down to its bare necessities: since the gods need nothing, he believed it was therefore godlike for us to need little. Once, for instance, when he was using a cup to collect water from a fountain, he noticed a young girl simply using her hands to scoop the water to her mouth. Diogenes smashed his cup to the ground in disgust and vowed to never again drink with such pointless extravagance. Cups are simply another way civilisation has wedged a gap between us and the earth, between our bodies and nature.

Though many Athenians were appalled by Diogenes, others admired him for living so frugally. One of his admirers, a rich man, once invited him to his house. Aware of Diogenes's poor manners, he begged Diogenes not to spit on anything valuable. Diogenes responded by turning to his host and spitting in his face. 'You're nothing valuable,' Diogenes said, and did it again.

Another time Alexander the Great visited Diogenes, whom he found sunbathing beside his barrel. 'The most powerful man in the world stands before you,' Alexander said.

Diogenes yawned.

'I deeply respect you,' Alexander continued. 'Ask of me anything and I shall do it for you.'

Diogenes looked up at the emperor and said, 'Could you get out of my light? You're blocking the sun.'

The onlooking crowd gasped at the impudence, but to Diogenes the title 'emperor' meant nothing. Titles and status are social inventions that have no place in the natural world (there is no king mouse or emperor flea).

The crowd eagerly awaited the philosopher's swift execution, yet it did not come. Alexander's admiration for Diogenes was only deepened by the encounter.

Following a rare invitation, Diogenes was once at a dinner party where the other diners noticed that he was eating with his dirty fingers. They called him a dog and threw their food scraps at him. He responded by standing up, raising his leg and urinating over them. 'If you call me a dog, I shall act like a dog,' he said, and sat back down barking.

This description of Diogenes as a dog is the reason he's now referred to as a Cynic (a word which derives from the Greek for dog) even though, as we saw above, he was first inspired by a mouse. The school of philosophy based on his ideas is called Cynicism.

Diogenes, like all Cynics, believed that a free life is the best life, and a free life is one that rejects social conventions. We shouldn't follow the norms and rules of society, we should simply follow our own nature. Rather than living to please others, Diogenes lived only to please his natural appetites. His embrace of nature and rejection of civilisation enabled him to live freely, and thus happily.

Many Athenians were troubled by his presence in their city and he faced the same hostility that immigrants still encounter today. He might, for instance, be minding his own business scratching his bum against a statue of Athena, and the natives would pass by and snarl, 'Oi, Diogenes, why don't you go home? Go back to where you came from!'

But such comments failed to upset him. 'I am a cosmopolitan, a citizen of the world,' he would reply. 'Athens is part of the world, therefore I *am* home.'

Diogenes did not see himself as belonging to any country; he had no allegiance or duty to anyone. He therefore rejected patriotism. His duties were not to his country or city but to himself, to nature.

When he tried to explain these ideas the Athenians often struggled to follow the logic of his arguments. 'Diogenes, I can't keep up,' they would protest. 'Philosophy is not for me.'

'Why live at all if you have no interest in living well?' he would reply.

He believed that befuddlement was essential to a good life. Philosophy for him was an exploration into questions of how we should live and what makes life good. To turn our backs on these questions is to turn our backs on life itself.

Finally, one day, after deciding he'd had enough of other people – 'scum,' he called them – he held his breath till he dropped dead, and that was the end of Diogenes.

10

Zhuangzi

Φ *Pronunciation* Jwong-za
Φ *Time* 369-286 BCE
Φ *Born* Meng (China)
Φ *Theory* Daoism

There is an ancient story told by philosophers known as 'Buridan's ass' about an idiotically rational donkey who starved to death. This donkey had made the following commitment: when faced with a decision it would weigh up each possible course of action and choose the most rational path. Pretty sensible, right? Well, not exactly...

One afternoon when the donkey was suddenly besieged by

hunger, it assessed its options and determined that the most rational course of action would be to look for food on a nearby farm, so off it went. Upon entering the farm it spied a large and enticing bale of hay out of the corner of its left eye. It was about to trot in that direction when it spied another bale of hay, just as large and enticing, out of the corner of its right eye. The donkey turned from left to right wondering what it ought to do.

Since both bales were equidistant from the donkey and contained the same quantity of equally delicious hay, it realised with some distress that it had no good reason to choose one bale over the other. But since it had decided to only ever pursue the most rational path, it was therefore paralysed. And so it just stood there, longingly turning from one bale to the other, growing hungrier all the time, till eventually it collapsed from starvation. What an ass!

For Zhuangzi this story perfectly illustrates the perils of reason. He believed that it was foolish to live a life governed by the rational assessment of possible actions; the joy and flow of life is bungled and botched by too much thought. Objectives, targets, aims and goals are all attempts to control the natural flow of things. They limit our ability for spontaneous, free action. As such, if success is a matter of achieving our goals, then for Zhuangzi success is the ultimate failure.

Rather than live like Buridan's ass, approaching every action with a methodical and detached assessment, we ought to act with openness and absorption. Consider the experience of playing an instrument. Mistakes occur when we start trying to plan and think about our fingers' movements, when we try to act as though we are the puppet masters of our bodies. To play well we need to abandon the division of mind over body, and body over instrument. Likewise, to live well, we need to act with open immersion in our situations, to trust ourselves and our abilities without always knowing how we are doing what we are doing.

To approach all situations like a musician, or tennis player, or carpenter, is to follow the *dao*, or 'Way'. The Way is what structures the unfolding rhythms of the universe. Using reason to distinguish between and evaluate possible actions upsets our spontaneous attunement to the Way.

Zhuangzi liked to express these ideas through stories. In one story he described how the philosopher Confucius was out for a walk when he noticed a person caught in the foamy tumult at the base of a waterfall. Fearing that the man had jumped in to commit suicide, Confucius rushed down to the bank, but was relieved to see him amble out of the water singing to himself.

'How did you stay afloat in such dangerous water?' Confucius asked.

'I go under with the swirls and come out with the eddies. I follow the Way of the water and never think of myself. That's how I stay afloat,' the swimmer replied.

The swimmer's skill arose from his lack of effort and will. He did not think of his survival as a battle between himself and the water. He did not try to dominate or conquer the water. Instead he formed an affinity with its violent whims.

Zhuangzi's own conversion to these ways of thinking occurred on one particularly bothersome day when he was out hunting. The bother started when a strange magpie with an enormous wingspan flew past him, brushing his forehead and landing in a chestnut grove. Zhuangzi was puzzled as to how this bird had failed to notice him with its large eyes. He followed it into the grove and took aim with his crossbow. As he was about to pull the trigger he noticed a cicada resting in a patch of shade, oblivious to a mantis hiding in the leaves behind it. The mantis darted forwards and snatched the cicada, but in that moment it forgot about its own vulnerability and was in turn devoured by the magpie.

Alarmed by this chain of ignorance – the cicada ignorant of the mantis, the mantis ignorant of the magpie, the magpie ignorant of Zhuangzi – he exclaimed, 'Each creature draws the other one into trouble.'

He now realised that he too had been ignorant of his surroundings and had wandered onto private land. He threw down his crossbow and fled, pursued by the keeper of the grove who yelled and cursed at him.

For the next three days Zhuangzi was in a foul mood. His narrow focus on the goal of capturing the magpie had caused him to lose awareness of his surroundings, just as the narrow concerns of the other creatures had caused them to lose sight of their surroundings.

He emerged from these gloomy days blessed with the understanding that he ought not to live a life obsessed with immediate gain, blinkered by the pursuits of his selfish wants. And these beliefs were further deepened after a fascinating conversation he had with an old skull.

Zhuangzi came across the ancient head lying in a hedgerow.

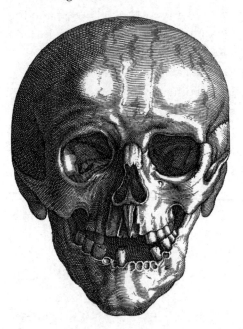

He struck it with his horsewhip in the hope that it might answer his questions. 'Good evening, sir, or madam,' he said. 'Tell me, what brought you to this fate? Was it war, or possibly execution? Were you taken by the cold or did hunger waste you away? Perhaps it was just the steady hammer of time that finally ground you down.' The skull was unresponsive.

Feeling tired Zhuangzi used the skull as a pillow and lay down to sleep. Then at midnight the skull appeared to him in a dream and said, 'You talk utter piffle, my friend. Yours are the questions of a person too tangled up in life's concerns. We dead have no interest in these questions. Would you like me to tell you about death?'

'Please do,' Zhuangzi replied.

'There is no authority among the dead. We have neither master nor slave, no rules to follow or enforce. There is no work to be done. We could not be happier.'

'This can't be true,' Zhuangzi protested. 'If I were able to resurrect you and return you to the world of the living, would you not welcome this?'

The skull frowned. 'Why should I wish to exchange my peace and happiness for life's burdens?'

Zhuangzi was delighted by the skull's words. He saw within them the possibility of a new way of life: to live as though dead, with the serenity of the happy skull. And so, when the king of Zhuangzi's province offered him the position of prime minister, he emphatically declined the wretched honour. A life of privilege, power and control is incompatible with the Way. Its vaulted ambitions, grand strategies and precise expectations sabotage the spontaneous flow of life. He compared it to the fate of a tortoise that is kept in a box and revered by a king. Would this tortoise rather be imprisoned, albeit honoured, or free, albeit trundling through mud? He had no doubt that the second option was infinitely better.

Thus Zhuangzi embraced a life of mud, working as a lowly sandal weaver, wearing an old patched gown and holey shoes held together by string. His face was pale and sickly. A life of carefree wandering does not come with riches. Poverty is the happy price of freedom. Emptiness is what enables us to follow the Way.

To illustrate the importance of emptiness in both belly and mind Zhuangzi told a story of a master carpenter who was asked how he managed to fashion such wondrous designs. The carpenter explained that he only began once he had achieved a state of stillness in which effort and energy were no longer necessary.

He achieved this state by fasting. After three days of fasting he no longer cared about payment. After five days he no longer cared about praise or criticism. Finally, after seven days, he forgot that he had a body and limbs – at this point his employer no longer existed and his body was able to work in unison with the Way of wood.

Emptiness allows us to travel through the world free from interference. When a person crosses a river and an empty boat bumps into his, he does not grow angry, but if the boat is occupied by someone, he shouts and rails. Likewise, if we drift through life with the emptiness of an unmoored boat, few people will bother us.

This is true for both emptiness and uselessness. The misshapen tree that proves useless to the carpenter will not be cut down. If we achieve a similar state of uselessness, no one will interfere with us. Only when we are of use to others are we pestered. Rather than live with calculated ambition or conscious striving, we should live intuitively and openly, allowing for the uncertainty of spontaneous action. In Zhuangzi's words:

I go nowhere and have no idea how I got there.

I go and come and don't know why.

I have no idea when my journey is over.

I wander and rest in infinite vastness.

Great knowledge comes in and I have no idea where it will all end.

Though the Way can be followed it cannot be intellectually

understood. It is beyond sight, sound and words. Invisible, inaudible, ineffable. We are only able to draw or illustrate what has shape, but the Way is the shaper of all things and is therefore itself unshaped. Since the Way can only be understood through action, static words cannot represent it. We use language to carve the world and distinguish *this* from *that* (this is a flower, that is a bird, this is a reptile, that is a mammal) but the Way exists beyond distinctions, and since it *things* everything, it is itself unthinged. Existing beyond language and concepts there are no questions that can be meaningfully asked about the Way. The ultimate truths of existence cannot be described or explained through words. They can only be lived.

Zhuangzi's belief that it is impossible to give an essential definition of the Way also meant that he was reluctant to give an essential definition of himself. One night, for instance, he dreamt that he was a butterfly fluttering through a bright meadow.

When he awoke the next morning he asked himself, 'Am I a man who dreamt he was a butterfly or am I a butterfly who now dreams he is a man?' Zhuangzi was happy to accept that neither option was the case. He simply moves spontaneously from one label – 'man' and 'butterfly' – to the next without seeking to determine a fixed essential truth.

Following the spontaneous transformations of the Way means that we neither resent nor regret our fate. Zhuangzi illustrated this with a story of a man who was surprised to see a willow tree inexplicably shoot out of his left elbow. Though somewhat inconvenienced by the new limb, he didn't complain or saw it off.

Zhuangzi himself exemplified this cool acceptance of fate when his wife died. Heard shortly afterwards singing happily and drumming on a pot, he was rebuked for not being sufficiently mournful.

'What is there to mourn?' he asked. 'Through the processes of change, from nothingness my wife found breath and a body, from then she was born, now through another change she has died. Like the passing of the four seasons, these are the ways of destiny. To regret her loss would mean to regret the very nature of things.'

He believed that it is wrong to think of death as the theft of what is rightfully ours; to die is not to have life stolen from us. Our life is not our possession. Our nature and destiny are not our property.

To possess life would be to possess the Way, which is a feat no more possible than possessing the wind.

When Zhuangzi was dying his followers wanted to give him an extravagant burial, but he objected. He simply wanted his body to be left out in the open.

'The heavens and the earth will be my coffin. The stars will be its pearls. How could this be bettered?' he asked.

'Master, we are afraid that the birds will devour your body.'

'Above ground I'll be eaten by crows, below ground I'll be eaten by worms. Why privilege the appetites of the latter?'

This was an instance of Zhuangzi exposing the foolishness of imposing distinctions – underground versus overground – where none are needed or applicable. The Way cannot be dissected with our human categories of right and wrong, life and death, you and me.

Since there are no distinctions there can be no judgments, and since there are no judgments there can be no arguments. If you judge that theft is wrong and I judge that it is right, what good can come of arguing about this? We cannot appoint an objective ruling from a neutral third person for this person will likewise judge us from their own position, and who's to say that their position is the correct one? Our judgments cannot determine the nature of things. They only describe how the nature of things appears from our chosen standpoint.

When his friends tried to argue with Zhuangzi, he would not respond analytically but playfully. While strolling across a bridge he once commented on the happiness of the fish in the river below. His friend objected, 'You are not a fish. How do you know that fish are happy?'

'You are not me. How do you know that I don't know the fish are happy?' Zhuangzi replied.

11

Pyrrho

Φ *Pronunciation* Pih-row
Φ *Time* 360-272 BCE
Φ *Born* Elis (Greece)
Φ *Theory* Scepticism

Pyrrho is the coolest person who has ever lived, though he wouldn't have believed it. That's because he didn't believe anything, and that's what made him so cool.

You see, though Pyrrho was widely admired during his lifetime, unusually for a philosopher it was not for what he thought or believed but for what he *didn't* think or believe – because he didn't think or believe anything. This intentional state of empty thoughtlessness was the source of his celebrity.

Does that mean he was famous for being stupid? Well, it's hard to say, after all, he *chose* to be stupid. Maybe choosing to be stupid is the smartest thing that anyone has ever done... or maybe it's the stupidest. Either way, what's certain is that living with an empty head made him extremely happy and relaxed about everything.

Pyrrho's descent (or ascent) into happy stupidity started with a long journey east. Having started his working life as a painter he gave it up in order to see the world by joining Alexander the Great on the conqueror's journey to India. While there he encountered a mysterious group of people who changed his life: the gymnosophists (naked wise men). These naked wise Indians told him something he would never forget, something that profoundly altered the way he lived.

Would you care to know what it was? So would I! You see, no one actually knows. It remains a mystery. But though we don't know precisely what the naked Indians said to Pyrrho, we do know the effect that it had on him.

To start with, on the journey back to Greece Pyrrho's ship was caught in a violent storm. Everyone on board was in a panic, fearing for their lives, except Pyrrho, who was unperturbed. With water gushing into the hull and sailors screaming for their lives, Pyrrho calmly sat clipping his toenails.

'Aren't you afraid, Pyrrho?' one sailor cried.

Pyrrho pointed to a pig that was also on board the boat happily eating its gruel, likewise indifferent to the danger. 'That is how we should live, like that pig,' Pyrrho said. He believed he had discovered the secret to the pig's happiness and was determined to implement this discovery into his own life, which led to rather curious behaviour.

When he returned to Greece he developed a habit of walking out into the middle of the road, oblivious to the oncoming traffic.

If it weren't for his friends keeping a close eye on him, he would have certainly been killed. Roads were not the only danger: they frequently had to pull him back from cliff edges too.

His friends were perplexed by his odd behaviour and quizzed him to find out why he was acting so recklessly.

'Are you trying to kill yourself, Pyrrho?'

'I really don't think so.'

'Well why do you walk so close to cliff edges?'

'Why not?'

'You might fall.'

'Might I? I don't know. I have no beliefs about this either way.'

'Have lost your mind?'

'Possibly. I don't know.'

Though he refused to write his thoughts down, Pyrrho's friends gradually understood why he was acting so strangely. It slowly dawned on them that he had become a sceptic.

Scepticism is the view that nothing can be known, and since nothing can be known, Pyrrho thought we shouldn't believe anything either. And so he had vowed to live without judgments, beliefs or opinions.

His friends tried to challenge these ideas.

'But surely you know that elephants are large!'

'Are they? I suppose they appear large to me, but to a blue whale, they're rather small. It depends on how you look at it. I have no beliefs about this either way.'

'But surely you know that tortoises are slow!'

'Are they? Their speed is considerable when compared with that of a growing tree. It depends on how you look at it. I have no beliefs about this either way.'

'But surely you know that Zeus is the highest of all gods!'

'Is he? The naked Indians I encountered on my travels had never even heard of Zeus. I have no beliefs about this either way.'

'But surely you know that you are a man!'

'Am I? The young lady who sleeps in a shrub called me a pigeon this morning. It depends on how you look at it. I have no beliefs about this either way.'

'She is insane! You shouldn't listen to her.'

'Maybe you are insane. Maybe I shouldn't listen to you.'

'You know perfectly well that I am sane.'

'Prove it. Do something that only a sane person would do.'

Pyrrho's friend was stumped.

'It seems reasonable to conclude that a person who struggles to do something sane is probably insane,' Pyrrho commented.

'You are ridiculous!'

'Am I? I have no beliefs about this either way.'

Pyrrho thought that the way to achieve ataraxy (peace of mind) was to avoid having beliefs (like the seafaring pig, whose contentment arose from its ignorance of death's proximity). Since knowledge is impossible we should give up trying to acquire it. We should suspend our judgments on everything. Scepticism makes us happier. Instead of becoming confused or arguing about things we will never know, we should free ourselves from all belief.

His sceptical attitude meant that he was very cool and calm about all things – some might say *too* calm and cool. Once when he was out walking he passed his friend who happened to be drowning in a swamp, but rather than stop to help his friend he simply strolled by whistling to himself.

'Don't you care if your friend dies?' he was later asked.

'I have no beliefs about this either way,' Pyrrho replied, but his drowning friend, who was eventually rescued, was not offended. In fact, he greatly admired Pyrrho for his actions (or inactions).

Another time Pyrrho was undergoing surgery – this was before the invention of anaesthetics – but he didn't scream or howl in pain. He calmly lay on the operating table whistling to himself.

'Isn't the pain unbearable?' his surgeon asked, while sawing his thigh open.

'I have no beliefs about this either way,' Pyrrho replied, rather predictably.

And if you asked him a question and then walked away, he would just carry on talking – it didn't bother him if no one was listening. Nothing bothered him. He was beyond bother. Beyond befuddlement.

The people of his hometown were so impressed with his breezy attitude to life that they made its philosophers exempt from taxation, but of course, it didn't make much of a difference to Pyrrho. He didn't care either way.

12

Epicurus

- Φ *Pronunciation* Eh-pih-cure-uss
- Φ *Time* 341-269 BCE
- Φ *Born* Samos (Greece)
- Φ *Quote* 'Let no one delay the study of philosophy while young nor weary of it when old. For no one is either too young or too old for the health of the soul.'

Epicurus was either a gluttonous lout who ate and drank to such excess that he threw up multiple times a day, or he was a figure of wonder and goodness, a man mightier than Hercules and more bountiful than a god. It all depends on whom you believe. These wildly conflicting views were expressed by different ancient writers. But who was telling the truth?

Well, the stories of putrid overeating are most certainly false.

In truth he was more of a nibbler than a gobbler, a man content to eat nothing more than a thin slice of cheese for supper. The stories of gorging and guzzling were probably invented by those who wished to sully his reputation: Epicurus certainly had his enemies.

Since the aim of his philosophy was to free us from anxiety and distress, it may seem odd that he should have provoked such vitriol. The problem, however, wasn't with his aims; it was with how he tried to achieve those aims. In order to overcome our anxieties Epicurus believe it was necessary to recognise the uncomfortable truth that we are alone in the universe, that there are no gods guiding or shaping our lives, that there's no meaning or purpose to our existence.

According to Epicurus the universe is nothing but a whirlwind of atoms and luck. Everything is merely a product of chance and accident. There is no use praying to higher beings for help, nor is there any prospect of us ever joining such beings in the afterlife. Death is the absolute end of our existence.

Though these ideas were intended to liberate us from irrational fears of divine wrath, many people found them hard to stomach; having sipped the Epicurean medicine they would spit it back out. For this reason one of Epicurus's devotees, a Roman called Lucretius (who was himself the target of slanderous lies, including a story that he went mad after taking a love potion), used poetry to present the philosophy. Like a spoonful of sugar he hoped that the pleasantness of the rhythm might sweeten the initial bitterness of the ideas.

The idea that there is no ultimate authority controlling the universe was one that Epicurus had no difficulty accepting; he was quick to discover the limitations of authority. When he was 12 years old he had a lesson at school on the origin of the universe according to the revered and ancient poet Hesiod. Though Hesiod's account was widely believed Epicurus struggled to understand it.

'We learn from Hesiod that in the beginning Chaos was born,' his teacher said.

Epicurus raised his hand. 'Everything born is born from something else, so how could Chaos be both the first thing and born? What was it born from?' he asked.

His teacher explained that he was incapable of answering such questions and that if he wished to study the nature of reality, he'd better go to talk to the philosophers, and so Epicurus did just that. He travelled across many different cities and spoke with many different philosophers, challenging them with his incisive questions.

From a philosopher named Nausiphanes he learned of the theory (first presented by Democritus) known as atomism. According to atomism everything in the universe is made of tiny indivisible entities known as atoms. These are the smallest things in the universe. Larger entities are formed through atoms combining in different ways. This theory had a profound impact on Epicurus and became the foundation of his philosophy.

At the age of 32 his own ideas and theories were developed enough that he started to teach. This experience then emboldened him to open his own school of philosophy near Athens, one that would rival other more prestigious and established schools, such as the Academy founded by Plato. Nestled among a grove of trees outside the city walls, Epicurus's school became known as the Garden.

The Garden was a community of friends united in their wish to live a tranquil life. Only those subjects capable of reducing anxiety were taught and discussed. Epicurus believed that the sole purpose of philosophy, and all intellectual endeavour, was to overcome suffering. If humans did not suffer, there would be no need for science or philosophy.

Unlike Pythagoras's community, the members of the Garden were not required to share everything and were free to have their own property. Epicurus believed that having your own property helps to build trust with others, which is vital for friendship. Analogously, possessing your own secrets allows you to form relationships on the basis of whom you share them with.

Unusually for the time and place, women and slaves were welcome at the Garden, and unlike Plato, who advised against studying philosophy before the age of 30, Epicurus also admitted children. He believed that no one was too young, or too old, for philosophy. Since philosophy for Epicurus was primarily a matter of attaining happiness, it was clearly of importance to people of all ages. And since Epicurus believed that marriage, family and politics disrupt our tranquillity, he advised his followers not to be involved in them.

At the heart of his philosophy was the atomist view that the universe is an endless void containing an infinite number of infinitely old and indestructible atoms. The universe has neither beginning nor end. It is eternal, without creator or destroyer. According to Epicurus, to destroy something involves breaking it down into smaller parts. Since atoms have no smaller parts (they are the smallest things), they cannot be destroyed. We, on the other hand, *can* be destroyed. This is because we are just bundles of atoms, and when those bundles break apart we cease to exist. There is no spiritual or non-physical part of us. We are flesh and bone, nothing more.

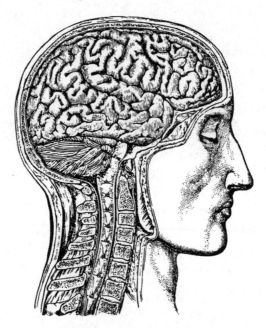

Epicurus felt this was a great source of relief. Since death is nothingness, and since it is irrational to fear nothingness, it is irrational to fear death. We need not dread the loneliness or pain of the afterlife. Moreover, feeling sad that we won't exist at some future time, Epicurus argued, is the same as feeling sad that we didn't exist in the past, and since we aren't troubled by our non-existence 200 years ago, nor should we be troubled by our non-existence in 200 years hence.

Though Epicurus did believe in gods, he believed that they did not involve themselves in the workings of the universe, which means we do not need to fear their judgment or anger. There is no design or purpose to anything that happens in nature. The animals, plants and rocks were formed through atoms swerving unpredictably and colliding with each other to form novel combinations. (Since Epicurus believed that we have free will, he was keen to stress this tendency of atoms to move randomly because in a world where atoms simply followed strict physical laws there could be no freedom.) The randomly formed combinations of atoms that fail to thrive fall to pieces, whereas those that function well continue. (This is similar to Charles Darwin's theory of natural selection, which was similarly anticipated by Empedocles's theory of roving limbs explored in chapter 4.)

Once anxiety and suffering have been removed, life is at its greatest. Epicurus believed that pleasure ought to be our ultimate aim in life, and that pleasure can simply consist of the absence of pain. Of course, there are active pleasures, such as eating and kissing, but since mere painlessness lasts longer than these fleeting pleasures, Epicurus thought we can be more confident of having a happy life by pursuing painlessness alone.

These beliefs make it clear that the stories of Epicurus's overindulgence are most certainly false. He lived a basic and frugal life. He went so far as to boast that with a slice of barley cake and cup of water, his bliss was as great as Zeus's. For Epicurus, the detached and untroubled lives of the gods are what we ought to aspire for.

Friends and philosophy help us achieve this godly state of serene happiness. This is why Epicurus lived among friends rather than family, and also why he wrote 300 books on philosophy, including *On Love*, *On Touch* and *On Fate*. It was owing to these texts that Lucretius compared him to a god. He believed that these gifts were greater than those of the gods, greater than, say, the gift of wine from Bacchus. And though Hercules defeated Hydra, the nine-headed water snake, and strangled the Nemean lion with his bare hands, Epicurus managed to vanquish a series of more formidable foes: our fears, anxieties and worries.

Unfortunately, despite his belief that pleasure is the ultimate aim of life, Epicurus died from kidney failure in agonising pain. Nevertheless, by focusing on the happy memories of former conversations he'd had with his friends, he remained in good spirits and described the day as blissful. He believed that the suffering of the mind is far greater than that of the body: so long as his mind was at peace, his physical pain was bearable.

Happily, then, at the age of 72, he drew himself a warm bath and there, in the comfort of its bubbles, he died.

13

Hipparchia

- Φ *Pronunciation* Hih-park-ee-ah
- Φ *Time* 340-280 BCE
- Φ *Born* Maroneia (Greece)
- Φ *Theory* Cynicism

To her parents' disappointment Hipparchia suffered from a condition commonly known as growing up. While a child she was dutiful, obedient and well mannered: everything they wanted in a daughter. But as she grew into a young woman she became wilful and strong-minded. She started to argue back and develop her own ideas about the world.

Hoping that marriage might soften her mind and revive her lost sweetness, her parents arranged for a number of young men to compete for Hipparchia's hand. They gathered the finest men in the city – men of noble standing, great beauty and bountiful wealth – but Hipparchia was dissatisfied with all of them.

'Why are you being so fussy?' her parents pleaded.

'I don't love any of these men,' she replied.

'*Love* – irrelevant! They are advantageous matches.'

'I refuse to marry a man I don't love.'

'You are our child and you will do as we say.'

'Why should I do as you say? Is it because possession entitles you to control?'

'Well, yes.'

'And are you not *my* parents?'

'Of course.'

'So it follows that you should do as *I* say.'

'What insolence! How dare you reason with us!'

'If reason is incompatible with politeness, then the problem lies with the latter, not the former.'

'Hipparchia, *please*, have mercy on us and just marry someone – *anyone.*'

After several months nothing had changed. Her parents were in despair. The city's stock of eligible suitors had been exhausted. But then, one bright and happy day, Hipparchia bounded home to tell her parents she had finally found the man of her dreams.

'Who is he?' they asked eagerly.

'I saw him in the market. He was surrounded by a crowd of people who were listening to him speak about freedom and life.'

Their hearts sank.

'Is the man of your dreams a *philosopher*?' they asked in disgust.

'Yes! A philosopher of the highest intelligence! He said that we ought to embrace our natural inclinations and live without shame.'

'Who is this man?'

'Crates.'

'The hunchback?!'

'Yes! The hunchback!'

'This is absurd. You cannot marry a philosopher, especially not a Cynic.'

'You said I could marry anyone,' she pointed out.

'Anyone *respectable*. We cannot consent to this.'

'It's too late. I've already asked him.'

'What?!'

'He said yes. Isn't it wonderful?'

'It's a catastrophe! We need to talk this through.'

'I'm afraid I've made up my mind. There's nothing more to say.'

'Hipparchia, darling, you're not being realistic. This man has no property or wealth, he has nothing to offer you.'

'Well of course he has: his exquisite mind. I find him absolutely fascinating! While listening to him I was filled with so many thoughts of my own. I too want to become a philosopher!'

'It's out of the question. We forbid it.'

'I had anticipated this,' she sighed, drawing a knife from her pocket. 'If I cannot live as I choose, I choose not to live,' she said, holding the blade to her throat. 'Farewell.'

'My goodness! Stop!' her parents pleaded.

'Will you permit me to marry Crates?'

'Yes, OK, but before you make this commitment, may we at least meet him?'

'That'd be lovely!'

The next night Hipparchia's parents sat down to supper with the philosopher. They looked on in astonishment as he ate with his fingers, dirtied his beard with crumbs and inadvertently extinguished the candles with an elephantine fart.

After dinner, while Hipparchia was out of the room, they pulled him to one side.

'Frankly, Crates, we're disgusted by you. We think it would ruin our daughter's life if she were to marry you.'

'I imagine it must be a source of great shame to have raised a daughter with a mind of her own.'

'We're so glad you understand,' they said, failing to detect his sarcasm. 'Please, try to dissuade her from this folly.'

'I shall do my level best,' he said.

At that moment Hipparchia re-entered the room, and to her shock, not to mention her parents' horror, Crates greeted her by removing his clothes.

'Hipparchia, here is everything I own. Plainly I am a man endowed with neither beauty nor wealth. The choice is yours.'

Hipparchia stood in silence while her parents waited with bated breath – surely, this pitiful sight would sour her affections. But their hopes were swiftly dashed when Hipparchia erupted into laughter, grabbed Crates by the hand and ran out of the house, never to return.

The next day the two were married. They celebrated wildly and without a shred of embarrassment, kissing and fondling in the middle of the street, indifferent to the stares of the gawping onlookers.

Their life continued in this way: a homeless existence of

talking and kissing and thinking and sleeping. And whenever her parents saw Hipparchia in the street, they looked the other way, acting as though they bore no relation to her.

Her parents were not alone in their disapproval. Indeed, this was a sexist society not accustomed to seeing women engage in philosophy. One evening the pair attended a party of philosophers. While they were mingling a man named Theodorus called out her name. The room fell silent as he approached her.

'Hipparchia, I have a hole in my cloak. Be a dear and mend it for me.'

'Excuse me?'

'I thought you may as well keep yourself busy while the men discuss philosophy.'

Hipparchia was unperturbed by this provocation. 'Theodorus, there's a matter of logic I've been struggling with,' she said coolly.

'Naturally,' he scoffed.

'Will you assist me?'

'I'd be honoured.'

'You and I, we're not equals, are we?'

'No more so than masters and slaves.'

'But you and my husband are equals?'

'That is correct.'

'And if you are equals, does it follow that you have the same rights?'

'That is also correct.'

'And do you have the right to punch Theodorus?'

'Well, of course, I *am* Theodorus!'

'Tell me, then, what conclusion follows from these premises?'

'Let's see now...'

He took a moment to work through the premises before saying, 'Ah, clearly the conclusion is that Crates has the right to punch me.'

'As I thought,' said Hipparchia. 'Darling?' And with that Crates socked Theodorus in the jaw, knocking him to the ground.

'Thank you for the logic lesson,' Hipparchia said.

Flushed with humiliation, Theodorus scrambled to his feet and in a rage pulled off Hipparchia's cloak (the only thing she was wearing).

Hipparchia looked down at her naked body. 'As you wish me to be,' she said, and carried on mingling.

'You have no shame!' Theodorus cried out.

'Thank you,' she replied, delighted by the compliment.

'How are we to discuss philosophy when she is walking about like this?' he said, appealing to the room.

'If you cannot control your thoughts while looking at my body, then the shame is yours, not mine.'

'You do not belong here. A woman's place is at the loom.'

'Poor man, you really are desperate for me to mend that hole in your cloak. Very well,' she said, and proceeded to rip his cloak completely in two. 'There, no hole!'

Theodorus yelped and scurried out of the room naked.

'Would anyone else care to educate me on where I belong?'

The room was silent, except for Crates, who was howling with laughter.

14

Jesus

Φ   *Pronunciation* Jee-zuss

Φ   *Time* 4 BCE-30 CE

Φ   *Born* Palestine

Φ   *Quote* 'You must therefore be perfect, as your heavenly Father is perfect.'

It may surprise you to learn that when Jesus was a child he once cursed another boy who promptly dropped dead. This was because the boy had angered Jesus by knocking into his shoulder as he ran by him. Terrified of his power and ill temper, the boy's bereaved parents asked Jesus's father to take his son and leave their village, so Jesus turned them blind.

This is what the *Infancy Gospel of Thomas* would have us believe. There are many unexpected stories about Jesus from the numerous ancient biographies of his life. But we're going to restrict our focus to the four most widely read accounts (known as the canonical gospels) which are included in the Bible: Matthew, Mark, Luke and John. Even among these four there are multiple inconsistencies and contradictions. They can't all be true, not entirely. There is no single correct version of his life.

In fact, some of the details we are most familiar with aren't actually described in the Bible. For instance, you may have heard that Jesus was born in a stable. Well, that's not true, at least it's not mentioned. The only building specifically mentioned is a house. You may have also heard that he was visited by three kings from the East. Again, that's not what we're told. They were magi (astrologers and occultists of the type that Pythagoras had visited hundreds of years prior to Jesus's birth) and there may well have been twelve, or twenty, or a thousand – we're not told. Two of the gospels don't even describe Jesus's birth. According to Mark and John there was nothing remarkable about his childhood. But let's forget who said what and start patching our story together.

Jesus's life started with the supernatural impregnation of his mother, Mary, by God. This wasn't a total surprise to her, for prior to the event an angel had appeared with the frightening news that she'd been chosen by God to perform this special honour. When her husband Joseph became aware of the pregnancy he assumed she'd committed adultery and resolved to divorce her, but an angel then visited him in a dream to explain who the father was, and so they remained married.

These angels were certainly helpful. Following Jesus's birth in Bethlehem Joseph was contacted by another dream-angel who informed him that Herod, the local king, feared he would one day be deposed by Jesus. To avoid this fate Herod ordered for every baby boy in Bethlehem and the surrounding area to be killed. Owing to Joseph's dream, however, he had already fled to safety with Mary and Jesus before the slaughter began.

The three of them eventually settled in a small town called Nazareth. Despite his extraordinary start to life Jesus had an uninteresting childhood. The first sign of his deep spiritual longing and the passion that would engulf the final years of his short life occurred during his early adolescence.

Being Jewish his parents would travel down to Jerusalem every Passover to celebrate the festival. However, at the age of 12, Jesus realised that he didn't want to leave. As the hordes of pilgrims trundled home, Jesus snuck back to the temple, a grand and awe-inspiring structure that dominated Jerusalem.

After a day's travel Mary and Joseph realised that he was missing from their caravan. Panic-stricken they retraced their steps in search of him. Was he lost? Had he been kidnapped? Would they ever see him again? For three days they were tormented by nightmarish possibilities. And so it was both a great relief and a shock when they finally found him sitting in the temple, safe, absorbed in conversation with teachers. He showed none of the distress of a lost child desperate for the comfort of his parents. On the contrary, the child they saw was full of energy and excitement, astonishing onlookers with his discerning questions and eagerness to discuss ideas on the higher purpose of existence, of how we ought to live, of what makes life good, and of whether a new and purer world was possible.

Caught in a confusion of sadness, gladness and anger, Mary begged Jesus to explain why he had left them. But Jesus didn't apologise. Instead he criticised his parents for not knowing where he was. It should've been obvious, he thought, that he answered to a higher authority: God. Despite his longing to stay, he compliantly returned to his ordinary, unthinking life.

For the next twenty years Jesus lived a quiet, simple life in Nazareth working as a carpenter, a trade he learnt from Joseph. However, his fervour to seek a new world and explore higher states of human perfection could not remain buried forever. They were finally and conclusively revived when Jesus heard news of a man named John who lived in the wilderness and taught of the world's imminent transformation by God.

John had renounced the comforts of ordinary life. He wore an uncomfortable shirt made of camel hair and lived on a meagre diet of locust and honey. With the coming of the new world he taught that it was necessary to repent for one's sins, and in the waters of the River Jordan he offered to cleanse people of their sins through baptism.

Inspired by the power and passion of John's teachings, Jesus escaped his quiet life in Nazareth to be baptised. He was so affected by the experience of baptism that instead of returning home he strayed into the desert alone. To prepare himself for the pursuit of higher ideals he wanted to overcome the tedious needs of the body, and so for forty days he resisted the urge to eat.

When he emerged from these trials in the desert he was informed that John had been sent to prison (where he would later be decapitated). Jesus thus decided to quit carpentry, leave Nazareth and continue John's mission of preaching repentance and the coming of a new world.

Living without an income, relying on the charity and generosity of others, he travelled from town to town, teaching on the nature of goodness and how we ought to live. Those who heard his teachings were astonished by both the newness and force of his words.

Jesus also found that he had the power to heal and drive out demons. In one town he healed a blind man by spitting in his eyes. In another he encountered a man who was possessed by a host of demons. This crazed man had the strength to tear off chains and spent his days stalking graveyards and cutting himself with stones. When Jesus released the demons from him they entered a herd of 2,000 pigs. Deranged, the pigs then bolted down a hill and ran headlong into a lake where they drowned. When the locals learnt of this incident they asked Jesus to leave.

Though many were enthused by Jesus's words and actions, some were troubled by them. Jesus's belief that love and compassion are the very substance of reality (a reality he called God) meant that he would pursue and prioritise them over human rules. It is, for example, traditional for Jews not to work on Saturdays (the Sabbath), but when Jesus saw a man suffering with a withered hand he ignored this tradition and healed him. Some who witnessed this were worried by Jesus's willingness to violate their norms. They even suspected that he was himself possessed by demons. Jesus, for his part, was dismayed by their shallowness.

His fame rapidly grew. Despite his wish to teach, he was solitary by nature. Solitude afforded him the opportunity to think and pray, to turn his heart to higher things, and he was easily angered by stupidity, which he saw everywhere, even among his followers. To try to contain and control his fame he implored those he met not to talk of him, but they rarely honoured his request, and soon crowds immediately gathered everywhere he went.

When his family heard the rumours of him they thought he'd lost his mind and tried to force him to return with them. But Jesus was no longer a child. He would not obligingly trudge back home as he had done as a 12-year-old. Now a man, he declared that they were not even his family. They had no claim over him. He told his followers that only those who hated their parents and siblings were worthy of being his disciples. We must discard our original selves and undergo a second birth. Family is merely a social institution that ceases to exist when viewed from the perspective of ultimate reality. Marriage, too, is a temporary feature of this life and not recognised by the eyes of eternity. When the new world arrives we shall become like angels and our human conventions will be forgotten.

He did at one point return to Nazareth, but it wasn't a happy homecoming. When the locals asked him to perform the same wondrous feats that he had performed elsewhere, he pointedly refused. He explained that his loyalty and devotion was to a higher reality, not to any particular town or people. Since he was essentially homeless on earth he owed them nothing. Infuriated by this slight they tried to throw him off a cliff, but he managed to escape.

Jesus wasn't surprised by their hostility. In fact, he declared that this was his aim. His project was not to create peace but division, to turn families against each other. Conflict is an inevitable consequence of turning away from our earthly attachments to pursue that which is both higher and infinitely more valuable: perfection.

Jesus longed for perfection. He called this perfection God. It is the true and eternal reality. It is what we ought to devote our lives to pursuing. It is the new world, the world that is coming, and only those who have lived in hope of it will be welcome. As humans we cannot achieve this perfection, but we ought to try. We ought to try to transcend our inescapable limitations. We ought to live in the radiance of this impossible demand.

This means accepting the fundamental truth that no one is good, everyone falls short. Pride is a failure to measure ourselves against the standards of perfection. To take perfection as our standard is to see ourselves as lowly, insignificant children. It is to feel no attachment to or satisfaction with our lives. It means living not to please or exhibit our goodness for the gaze of imperfect humans.

To live in pursuit of perfection, for the gaze of an all-knowing God, means striving to ensure that not only our actions but our thoughts are pure and good. This is why Jesus and his disciples made a point of not washing their hands before eating; they wanted to illustrate that it is what is already within us – malicious thoughts, wicked feelings, sinful inclinations – that is the source of our real uncleanliness. It is foolish to worry about keeping our bodies free of pollution when the real impurities are already inside.

It is not enough to refrain from lashing out or losing our temper. We should aim to rid ourselves of angry feelings. We should regard an angry thought as no less wicked than an angry deed. Likewise, Jesus believed that an adulterous act is no worse than an adulterous thought; the thought and the deed are one and the same, both equally wrong. In order to undertake this mission of self-purification we must stop striving for worldly goods such as money. Money is a concern of the flesh, not the spirit.

The demand for perfection meant that following Jesus was a considerable challenge. He required his followers to leave their families and give away all their possessions, even their sandals. Preparing for the new world means living as though you are not of this world. Those who are happy with their lives now are not worthy of the world to come. The rich and well-fed are ultimately destined for poverty and starvation. Only those who ignore the infinite demands of perfection's call have the time to amass wealth and property.

When Jesus entered Jerusalem with his disciples for Passover he watched in dismay as they marvelled at the size and grandeur of the temple. He explained that for all its magnificence the temple will not last. It will be torn down and pass away with this world. Upon entering the temple his exasperation only grew, for there inside were stalls with pilgrims exchanging different currencies of money so that they could purchase animals for sacrifice to God.

In Jesus's eyes the process of worship had been turned into a transaction. This sacred space had been contaminated with the bustle and clamour of a market. Rather than the temple elevating the minds of pilgrims to contemplate the perfection of God and the world to come, they were instead dragging the temple down

into gutter of their everyday conventions and concerns. It was as though they believed they could purchase their salvation, that the quest to save their souls was merely a matter of performing a few rituals rather than wedding every passing second to a life of love.

Jesus was sickened by what he saw. He was so utterly fed up with the stupidity and shallowness he found everywhere around him that in a fit of rage he made a whip out of cords and chased the animals and money changers out of the temple. He then tossed over their tables and scattered the coins across the ground.

Unfortunately for Jesus this scene did not escape the attention of the watchful Roman guards. Jerusalem was part of Judea, which at this time was a Roman province. The Jews were deeply unhappy with their subjugation by the Romans and the possibility of revolt simmered beneath the surface, liable to boil over at any moment. Owing to this volatility the Romans were swift to execute any individuals who might lead or incite an insurrection. And so it seems likely that when they saw the disorder in the temple being caused by a charismatic Jew accompanied by a clan of devout followers, they identified Jesus as a potential revolutionary leader. By the orders of the local prefect Pontius Pilate they therefore elected to kill him.

Jesus sensed the end was near. His final night was filled with anguish. He knew what the Romans did to rebels – crucifixion – and prayed to God to be spared this fate. But the next morning, with his location revealed to the Romans by the traitor Judas, one of Jesus's own followers, Jesus was arrested, tried and convicted.

The Roman soldiers mocked and beat him. They placed a crown of thorns on his head – ridiculing him for the crime they had charged him with, wishing to be 'king of the Jews' – and spat on him. They then led him to a hill outside of the city walls, nailed his wrists to a cross and left him to die.

It took six hours for the weight of his body to crush his lungs. In the moments before his death the sky darkened and he called out to God in desperation, 'My father, my father, why have you forsaken me?' But no answer came, and with his final breath he let out an agonising cry. As his head slumped forwards an earthquake struck, shattering the tombs of various holy men who then rose from the dead and wandered through the streets of Jerusalem.

Jesus's body was laid to rest in a tomb which was sealed by a large stone. But the next day, when three of his female followers arrived at sunrise to anoint the body, they found that the stone had been rolled away and the tomb was empty. A mysterious young man who was sitting beside the tomb said, 'Do not be alarmed. He is not here. He has risen! Go and tell his disciples of the news.'

Trembling and bewildered, the three women ran away, and they told no one of what happened.

15

Seneca

Φ *Pronunciation* Sen-i-ka
Φ *Time* 1 BCE-65 CE
Φ *Born* Cordoba (Spain)
Φ *Theory* Stoicism

Seneca hated emotions, which meant he also hated his hatred of emotions, which meant he also hated his hatred of his hatred of emotions. We could go, and on, and on. This is the problem with emotions. They're liable to get carried away. They don't know when to stop. They're just not sensible.

Instead of hatred, Seneca aimed for and favoured an attitude of reasonable disapproval. He wanted every aspect of our lives to be ruled by reason. We should, for instance, replace fear with measured caution, grief with rational acceptance, and anger (the savage desire for vengeance) with an effective plan to overcome the wrongs we endure.

Reason – our ability to think ahead, look back, calculate, act with care, exercise good judgment – is, among mortal beings, unique to humans and therefore our finest attribute. It raises us above the beasts of the earth. It is also the force that governs the universe. Every aspect of nature, from the migration of birds to the movement of the planets, is ordered and rational. Our human ability to likewise behave orderly and rational makes us godlike. We can regulate and control our lives as God regulates and controls the universe. Those who submit to emotion are forsaking their greatest power.

Emotions are the enemy of reason, and thereby of humanity itself. These febrile states of mind force us to act against our better judgment. Annihilation is the only solution. Merely trying to moderate our emotions is not enough. According to Seneca the idea of a moderate emotion is as ludicrous as that of moderate insanity or moderate evil. Any disturbance to reason is intolerable.

Given these beliefs, what sort of life do you imagine Seneca led? Do you envisage a quiet life, a serene life, a life without drama or incident? Well, this certainly was not the case. In reality Seneca occupied a place at the violent, brutal heart of Roman power. He was first a tutor and later an adviser to the notorious emperor Nero, an emperor who – despite Seneca's expressed belief that cruelty is utterly inhuman – will forever be remembered for poisoning his stepbrother, murdering his mother and torturing the innocent for entertainment. Clearly there were no personal bonds that would ensure one's safety against Nero's wrath and ultimately Seneca too died at his command.

Though he could not have foreseen this bloody end, it was Seneca's father who encouraged his son's career in politics. Born in a Roman colony in Spain – the empire during Seneca's lifetime would stretch from southern Britain to the Euphrates in Western Asia – Seneca was sent by his father at a young age to live with his aunt in Rome where he received a thorough education in rhetoric and grammar. Such an education was regarded as necessary training for budding politicians. But it was philosophy, not politics, that truly excited him.

His appetite to learn philosophy was so great that he was the first to arrive at school and the last to leave. Outside of lessons he would accost his philosophy teacher with questions whenever they happened to cross paths. Seneca saw this teacher as higher than a king, and so when he lectured on the evils of overindulgence Seneca dutifully vowed to never again eat oysters, or drink wine, or wear cologne, or sleep on soft pillows. And when another of his philosophy teachers lectured them on the various reasons for vegetarianism, including Pythagoras's belief in our kinship with animals (see chapter 1), Seneca gave up meat.

This final act of philosophical devotion, however, worried

Seneca's father. Around this time thousands of young men had been expelled from Rome for following non-Roman religious beliefs and practices. Seneca's father was concerned that his restricted diet might be misconstrued as a sign that he was a follower of Jewish or Egyptian religions. And so for the sake of his safety Seneca resumed eating meat. This didn't fully satisfy Seneca's father, however, who was suspicious of his son's love of philosophy. Little did he realise how vital it was to his well-being.

Throughout his life Seneca suffered from a debilitating lung condition (probably tuberculosis). As a child he felt able to endure the condition and had the willpower to fight it. But as he grew into a young man the disease gained the upper hand. His suffering intensified and he became dangerously thin. His life grew so difficult that he often considered ending it, but he worried about the effect this would have on his aging father.

It was friendship and philosophy that gave him the strength to live. By energising and exercising his mind, philosophy sustained Seneca's mental strength, which thereby eased the suffering of his body. But the remedial power of philosophy could not fully cure him of his condition, and so in the hope that a warmer climate might restore his health Seneca travelled with his aunt to Egypt and remained there for about 10 years, absorbing himself in the study of natural phenomena such as the passing of comets and the flooding of the Nile.

When Seneca returned to Rome he was finally ready to embark on a career in politics. Within a few years his impressive oratorical skills had made him famous within Rome. But these very talents nearly led to his execution.

The emperor at this time, Caligula, an insomniac who rarely slept for more than three hours a night, was quite possibly deranged. He would hold animated conversations with a statue of the god Jupiter, dress up as the goddess Venus, have anyone who looked down at his balding head executed and planned to appoint his horse to the senior position of consul. He once led the Roman army on a lengthy expedition only to stop them at the English Channel and order the troops to fill their helmets with seashells to take back to Rome; 'spoils of the ocean,' he called them, as though he had achieved some sort of victory over the sea.

Violent jealousy was another dimension of his mental instability. He once had a man executed simply because he was jealous of his fine clothes and chic haircut. Similarly, when he one day heard Seneca deliver an impressive speech in the senate, he ordered for him to be put to death. Fortunately for Seneca, the emperor was informed that his feeble health meant he would soon die anyway. Caligula was content to let nature serve as the executioner.

In the year 41 Caligula was assassinated, but this was no great boon to Seneca who, under the new emperor Claudius, was charged with adultery (with Caligula's sister, Julia Livilla) and exiled to the rocky island of Corsica. With the death of his son occurring only months before his banishment, this was a particularly difficult year for the philosopher. Nevertheless, he enjoyed the opportunity to be away from the frenetic pace of Roman life and spent his eight years in exile reading, thinking and writing.

After Claudius married Agrippina, another of Caligula's sisters and Claudius's own niece, Seneca was recalled to Rome. Agrippina wanted to prepare her son Nero for the role of emperor and hoped that Seneca's reputation as a philosopher would improve the public's perception of him. Seneca, moreover, possessed great skills of rhetoric and declamation which he could instil in Nero. She was insistent, however, that philosophy should form no actual part of the boy's curriculum. By this point Seneca had published his philosophical theories on and against anger; Agrippina evidently believed that exposure to such ideas would weaken Nero's prospects.

According to Seneca the quest to purge ourselves of emotions, especially anger, was necessary not only for our own good but for the good of humanity. He said that no plague had cost the human race more. It has led to the destruction of cities and the ruin of nations. It is the most hideous – Seneca bemoaned the ugliness of anger, with its 'threatening look' and 'gloomy countenance' – and frenzied of all the emotions, and it is a complete violation of our human nature. Human life rests upon kindness and cooperation. We exist for mutual assistance not mutual destruction.

Every night before he slept Seneca underwent a process of thorough self-reflection. He would identify those moments in the day when anger had taken hold of him and would consider how to avoid such moments in the future; for instance, he might instruct himself to ignore slights, or to respond with laughter instead of rage, or, when denied a place of honour at the dinner table, to simply not worry about silly social codes of honour and respect.

Seneca's commitment to rational self-assessment and wish for self-improvement was certainly not typical of emperors. Caligula, indeed, was fond of saying, 'Let them hate me, so long as they fear me.' If, for the sake of control, it is necessary to induce an irrational state of fear in the people, perhaps Agrippina believed an equally irrational predisposition towards anger was required to induce this fear. Whatever the reason for her opposition to philosophy, Agrippina would herself become a victim of Nero's intemperance.

Nero was not yet a man when he became emperor. Following Claudius's assassination – many believe Agrippina murdered him with poisoned mushrooms – the 16-year-old Nero, as Claudius's adopted son, became the youngest ruler the Western world had ever seen, and Seneca was suddenly promoted from a mere tutor to *amicus principis*, 'friend of the emperor'.

During the early years of Nero's reign Seneca published an essay entitled *On Mercy* in which he instructed the young emperor to rule not with cruelty but kindness and compassion. He argued that to save people from death is to exercise the power of a god; to destroy them is merely to act with the power of a fire or collapsing building. But these words came too late. The violence had already begun.

Britannicus failed to survive even the first year of his stepbrother's reign. It was his misfortune to have a singing voice more beautiful than Nero's and to be the biological son of Claudius. The first misfortune inflamed Nero's resentment of him and the second made Nero fear that the people would see him as Claudius's true successor. Nero therefore arranged to have the 13-year-old poisoned at a family dinner.

During this bloody banquet a hush descended when the diners noticed that Britannicus was struggling to breathe and unable to speak. Nero casually told the party that it was perfectly ordinary for Britannicus to have such fits, but it was clear to everyone what was happening. With no one brave enough to contradict the emperor, they returned to their meals, doing their best to ignore the mouldering corpse at the table.

Seneca was evidently able to overlook Britannicus's murder. He wasn't sufficiently troubled to request permission to step down as Nero's adviser and speech writer. During these early years, despite his former philosophy teacher's lectures against overindulgence, Seneca was busy amassing vast amounts of wealth and land. His position meant that he was the frequent recipient of gifts from those wanting influence or access to Nero. Added to the land directly gifted to him from Nero, Seneca thus became the owner of estates in Egypt, Spain and Italy, each with gardens famed for their size and magnificence. He added to these riches by loaning money at interest and selling the wine produced on his vineyard.

With his wealth, literary success (in addition to philosophical works he also wrote plays, most of which were bloody; *Thyestes*, for instance, is a play about the rivalry between twin brothers that ends with one brother tricking the other into eating his own children) and political position, Seneca was one of the most famous figures in the Roman empire. If the death of Britannicus wasn't wicked enough for him to renounce all that he had acquired, would the murder of Agrippina cause the writer of *On Mercy* and *On Anger* to shun his lofty position? No, it would not. And in this instance Seneca was not a passive bystander but an active participant in the plot.

Nero had grown tired of Agrippina's constant criticisms of him. She was forever meddling in his business, trying to influence his political decisions, seeking to manipulate him, so he decided to have her killed. His initial plan of engineering her bedroom ceiling to collapse on her while she slept failed, and so he devised an even more elaborate scheme. He ordered a ship to be built that would break apart when a lever was pulled, thus simulating a shipwreck.

But this plan also failed. Though the ship did break apart, Agrippina managed to swim to the safety of nearby boats. Nero was given news of her escape and feared she might gather her supporters to seek vengeance or expose his crime to the senate. He summoned Seneca to seek his counsel, and it was following this meeting that Nero dispatched a trio of assassins to finish the job.

Agrippina was no fool. She knew that the shipwreck was designed to kill her and so when the assassins arrived she understood their purpose. As the first sword was drawn from its sheath Agrippina asked that it be plunged into her womb, the place from where her monstrous son had entered the world.

Seneca wrote a letter on Nero's behalf to the senate presenting the false story that Agrippina had attempted to have the emperor assassinated and that her death was a fair punishment for this betrayal. The story failed to convince the senate who were duly appalled by Seneca's feeble attempt to deceive them.

With his mother dead Nero felt free to end the marriage she had arranged between him and Octavia, his stepsister. He had long been bored of her and was eager to marry another woman named Poppaea. Octavia was therefore exiled from Rome and subsequently executed. (Nero also made sure to execute those who expressed disapproval of his new marriage.) Despite being a marriage of his own choosing, this one ended no less brutally than his first. He killed Poppaea after she complained one night that he had come home too late.

The bodies were piling high in the court of Nero, and Seneca was desperate to retire before his own time was up. Though the emperor refused to officially sanction his retirement Seneca withdrew from political life and started to devote more time to philosophy. Closing your door on a fire, however, will only buy you time, and Seneca's days were numbered.

Almost as if Rome could no longer contain the tension and enveloping dread caused by Nero's reign, in the year 64 a real fire broke out and ravaged the city for nine days, destroying most of the buildings. A rumour spread that Nero had started the conflagration in order to raze the city and erect a new one in his name. He needed a scapegoat, someone he could blame to deflect these rumours. That misfortune fell to a religious sect known as Christianity which had newly emerged in Rome. Nero held the Christians responsible and as a punishment for the crime (the crime, that is, of being unfamiliar in their practices and beliefs) he had many of them torn apart by dogs. Others were soaked in a flammable substance and turned into human candles to illuminate the night.

The following year it was Seneca's turn to confront his fate. Nero had learnt of a plot against his life, but with little evidence of who was involved in the conspiracy he indiscriminately ordered executions. Many innocent people were sentenced to death, including Seneca. The years of support that Nero had received from Seneca were immaterial to him. No one was safe. And so it was that one morning during the year of 65, Seneca was awoken by a troop of Nero's soldiers who informed him that he had been ordered by the emperor to kill himself.

Seneca received the news without sadness. He had long admired the stories of Socrates' calm and stolid death and saw it as an honour to die in a similar vein. His wife also chose to die alongside him; however, Seneca was assailed by a swell of grief at the sight of her suffering. Fearing the emotional weakness might threaten his resolve he had her moved to another room (where her death was averted).

Seneca's death was not nearly as swift as Socrates'. His frailty meant that he was almost too deathly to die. Blood feebly trickled out of his opened veins and the hemlock he downed passed through his body as though it were a lifeless drain. The end eventually came after he was carried into a hot bath where he choked to death on the steam.

Questions & Activities

Though the stories have been told, the rest is not silence. It is now your turn to explore the ideas of the previous 15 chapters. Below is an array of questions and activities related to or inspired by our philosophers. With luck these will plunge you into your own whirlpools of befuddlement and release your own powers of thought.

Some of the ideas are presented using an argument structure with numbered premises that lead to a conclusion, so before you start let's familiarise ourselves with these. In an argument every numbered point is known as a premise. These combine to produce the final numbered point, which is the conclusion. Arguments can fail for two reasons: one or more of their premises aren't true, or when combined they don't actually produce the conclusion.

Consider the following argument:

1. Every star is made of snow.
2. The sun is a star.
3. Therefore, the sun is made of snow.

This argument fails for the first reason: though the combined premises do produce the conclusion, the first premise isn't true.

Let's consider an argument that fails for the second reason:

1. Every adult was once a baby.
2. I am an adult.
3. Therefore, Plato was Greek.

Even though the premises and conclusion are true, this is a bad argument because the conclusion does not follow from the premises, which is another way of saying that it has bad logic.

Let's fix its logic:

1. Every adult was once a baby.
2. I am an adult.
3. Therefore, I was once a baby.

This is now a good argument: its premises are true and the logic works. Have these two criteria in mind when thinking about the arguments presented below.

Pythagoras

Questions

- Pythagoras said, 'Friends should hold all things in common for friendship is equality.' But is this possible? Can we hold *all* things in common? Can we, for instance, share sleep or hunger? Can you think my thoughts? Can I experience your experience?
- If sharing is necessary for friendship, does that limit who we can be friends with? If there were two creatures who were so different that their wants and needs didn't overlap in any way, and who were therefore unable to share anything, would friendship between them still be possible? The philosopher Thomas Aquinas thought not. He believed that a shared language of some sort was necessary for friendship and that it is therefore absurd to speak of friendship with a horse 'for a certain mutual love is requisite and this is founded on some kind of communication'.
- Pythagoras believed that everything was made out of numbers, which raises the question: what are numbers made out of? Are they made out of anything? If something is made out of nothing, does that mean it *is* nothing? Is it

possible for a thing to simply be made out of itself?

Before we can even question what they are made of, we should perhaps first find out *what* they are. Consider the number 3. Is this the number 3 right here on the page? When you touch the page are you touching the number? Given that I've typed it more than once, does that mean it's in two different places at the same time? Or is it the case that 3 is not the number itself but the representation of the number? Are 3 and III the same thing or do they *refer* to the same thing? If the latter, *what* exactly is this thing they refer to? *Where* is this thing?

- If everything is made out of numbers, then everything can be quantified. But can our emotional and conscious states be quantified? For example, would it make sense to describe a sensation as 3.5x more pleasurable than another sensation? Would it make sense to say that this person is experiencing 5.42x more grief than that person?

The playwright George Bernard Shaw rejected a quantitative understanding of feelings and emotions. He wrote, 'What you yourself can suffer is the utmost that can be suffered on earth. If you starve to death you experience all the starvation that ever has been or ever can be... Poverty and pain are not cumulative... If you can stand the suffering of one person you can fortify yourself with the reflection that the suffering of a million is no worse.'

Shaw's idea of pain is rather like the property tastiness. A bowl with one profiterole contains just as much tastiness as a bowl with twenty; the tastiness of a single profiterole holds within it all the profiterole-tastiness that can be tasted on earth.

Is Shaw right to think of suffering in this way?

- Let's consider possible arguments for Pythagoras's dualism. Do any of them work? (The first two, though similar, are different, with the first focusing on the concept of persons and the second on the concept of thoughts.)

1. Bodies can be halved.
2. But people cannot be halved: there is no such thing as half a person (if a woman gave birth to a girl without legs and arms, though the body has parts missing, she is still a *whole* daughter and not *part* daughter).
3. Therefore, people are not their bodies.

1. Bodies can be chopped into little pieces.
2. But thoughts cannot be chopped into little pieces.
3. Therefore, thoughts are not part of our bodies.

1. I can doubt that my body exists (it's possible that it's merely an illusion).
2. I cannot doubt that my thoughts exist (their existence is immediate and undeniable).
3. Therefore, my thoughts (and the mind they comprise) are separate to my body.

1. Without my awareness you could find out everything about my body.
2. But unless I tell you, you will never know my thoughts and feelings.
3. Therefore, my thoughts and feelings are separate to my body.

1. My body is always changing.
2. But I essentially remain the same person.
3. Therefore, I am separate to my body.

1. If I were to drown, I would immediately cease to exist.

2. But my body wouldn't immediately cease to exist.

3. Therefore, I am not the same as my body.

1. Your body is an object.

2. You are not an object.

3. Therefore, you are not your body.

- Let's suppose that Pythagoras was right about the heavenly music of the orbiting planets. If he'd stopped being able to hear the music, would the sound have ceased to exist? Does it make sense for there to be a sound that absolutely no one can hear?

Activities

- Pythagoras's claim that the animals we encounter may have been friends or family from former lives is an interesting idea, but is it one we can viscerally and wholeheartedly believe? Look an animal – maybe a pet, prowling fox or wandering crow – in the eye. Can you feel a kinship with it? Is it possible to experience an intimacy between you as though you were once friends or even family? Or is there an unbridgeable gulf?

  Similarly, can you look at yourself in the mirror and regard yourself as not fully human? Can you see beyond your present form to spot the glimmer of a non-human essence? Do your eyes convey the presence of a being that existed prior to this life and this body?

Heraclitus

Questions

- Heraclitus believed that everything is in a constant process of becoming its opposite. But does everything have an opposite? Is there an opposite for each of the following:

- The present
- Religion
- God
- Eating
- Laughter
- Dancing
- Writing
- Blood
- Skin
- Jam
- Milk
- Thoughts
- The universe
- Spiders

- Heraclitus believed that to be alive is to be dying. Is this true? Are we dying all the time? Is this a pessimistic view of life?
- He also believed that to be awake is to be tiring. Is this true? Is it possible to be in a state of pure wakefulness?
- Heraclitus thought that everything in existence, including you, is essentially made of fire. Of the four categories (sometimes known as the four elements) earth, air, fire and water, which do you think best characterises the nature of the universe?

Activities

- Heraclitus thought that everything is in a process of constant change. Try to see whether you can find anything that is entirely still and changeless. For instance, can you hold a thought entirely still?

- He also thought that opposites are bound together. Try to experience a Heraclitean state of contradiction: walk round in a circle while looking over your shoulder. Are you both looking in front of and behind you? Are you simultaneously moving away from and towards your current position?

- Stay up till dawn to watch the sun rise. From your window observe the transition from night to day, from black skies to blue, and ask yourself: am I watching the replacement (as Hesiod thought) or the transformation (as Heraclitus thought) of the night?

- Heraclitus's solitary life in the mountains left him feeling despondent. Though he enjoyed playing childish games, would this have been possible alone? Test the limitations of solitude by trying to tickle yourself. Can you do it? No? Not even with the tip of your tongue across the roof of your mouth? Can you play-fight alone by pushing yourself over? Can you chase yourself? Even if these aren't possible, is one of the consolations of solitude that it's impossible to be immoral? Does total isolation render you faultless? Can you, for instance, lie to yourself? Or steal from yourself?

Zeno of Elea

Questions

- Zeno's first paradox follows his belief that space can be infinitely divided, but is this true? Is it possible that there is a minimum distance which cannot be divided any further? Could you, for instance, be shrunk infinitely? Or would you reach a limit, a point of maximum smallness (minimum largeness)?

- Zeno believed that we shouldn't trust our senses. They seem to tell us that objects can move, but according to Zeno logic tells us this is impossible. When there is a conflict between logic and our experiences, which should we trust?

  Logic tells me that for every single thing in the universe $x = x$ (everything is itself). It also tells me that nowhere in the universe is there a colourless red object or a 20-year-old teenager. This is despite the fact that I have not experienced every single thing in the universe; I've not traversed the cosmos. Does the ability of logic to reveal such universal facts that transcend our experience show it is better at discovering truth than experience?

- If Zeno was right that motion is an illusion, how significantly does this change our understanding of the world? If, for instance, there are certain entities whose essence is motion, then presumably they don't really exist.

  The wind might be such an entity. Should we say that wind *has* motion or *is* motion? In a world without motion, would wind still exist?

  Perhaps *we* are other such entities. Should we say that you *have* motion or *are* you motion? Do you *undergo* change or *are* you change? Imagine yourself as a statue. Imagine that you never moved again and remained this way forever, without a heartbeat or blood flow, without change or growth. Would you still exist?

- While Zeno believed we are deceived by the illusion of motion, could it in fact be true that we are deceived by the illusion of stillness? For instance, if everything in the universe were continuously becoming 1000x smaller with every passing second, would we know that this was happening? Is it possible to detect shared and collective changes? Or is it the case that if everything changes together, nothing really changes at all?

Activities

- Perhaps the illusion of motion isn't actually that hard to fathom. Perhaps we experience this illusion all the time. Ask a friend, a philosophical accomplice, to hold a ball and walk the breadth of the room holding it.

  Though the ball has seemingly travelled from one point in space to another, did it actually move or was the ball in fact stationary?

  We could apply the same questions to your nose. If I were to watch you from the sun, I'd see your nose hurtling through space at 67,000 miles per hour (the speed of the earth in its orbit), but is your nose actually moving or is this merely the illusion of motion?

Empedocles

Questions

- If Empedocles was right that the universe is either in a state of growing unity (under the force of love) or increasing disintegration (under the force of strife), which stage of the cycle do you think we're now in? What do your observations about the world indicate: are things coming together or falling apart?
- Could Empedocles's fundamental forces – love and strife – affect all things? For instance, could they affect time? Can time fall apart? Can it coalesce? Is it made of parts?
- The force of love induces a process of coalescence where everything mixes and merges. How easy is this to imagine? Can you imagine bodies merging? Can

one body become two people? Can one body have two minds?

Let's consider these questions in relation to the ancient Greek tale of Hermaphroditus.

Hermaphroditus was blessed with great beauty. No one could deny it. No one was immune to his radiance. Wherever he went he was the cynosure of attention. But on one strange and fateful day he crossed paths with the nymph Salmacis, and forever after, though he still turned heads, it was for an altogether different reason.

Much of that day had been unremarkable. He had hunted deer, as he often did, and the summer heat had been intense, as it often was. And after several hours of toil he had grown hot, weary and desperate to cool off. While in search of a lake he passed through a glade where he saw Salmacis in the centre singing to herself and dancing.

'Excuse me,' he said.

'Sorry, not today, very busy, thank you, bye-bye,' she replied, without so much as looking at him.

'Please, I don't mean to bother you. I'm trying to find a lake.'

Annoyed at his persistence, Salmacis stopped with the firm intention of giving him what for.

'Now who do you think you – oh my...'

At the sight of his gorgeous face her anger vanished.

'Do you know of a nearby lake?' he asked.

'Honey, baby, forget the lake – I've got other ideas for you.'

Hermaphroditus, realising that Salmacis would be of no use, turned to leave, but she, not known for her self-restraint, grabbed him by his tunic, pulled him towards her and growled, 'MARRY ME!'

He tried to recoil, but her grip only tightened. 'MARRY

ME!' she repeated, and started to lick his face.

'Get off!' he cried, pulling away, 'I don't want to marry you! I don't want to marry anyone.'

Salmacis, who was prone to mood swings, became suddenly contrite.

'So sorry! I don't know what came over me. Though, may I at least carry on licking you?'

'No! Leave me alone.'

'Fair enough,' she shrugged.

Hermaphroditus continued on his way, but the story doesn't end there.

Though Salmacis wanted to honour his request, she also found him utterly irresistible, and so, as a compromise, opted to follow him in secret while telling herself, 'Look but don't touch!'

This worked for a while. For close to an hour she was content just to stare and wish. However, when Hermaphroditus finally reached the lake he made the grave mistake of removing his clothes.

Salmacis's jaw hit the ground. She wrapped her arms around a tree to try to control herself. As his naked body glided through the limpid water, she repeated over and over, 'Look but don't touch! Look but don't touch!' But this was more than she could bear. Beating her head, grinding her teeth, rocking backwards and forwards – she realised that the only way to stop this madness was to give into it.

Moments later Hermaphroditus's peaceful swim was interrupted by a wild commotion near the shore. Looking over his shoulder he saw Salmacis speeding towards him. He swam away, aiming for the other side of the lake, but the distance between them rapidly closed, for where he had only fear to impel him, Salmacis was driven by a greater force, desire.

It wasn't long before she was able to reach out and grab his ankle. She pulled him towards her, reeling him in like a fish. He tried to get away but she wrapped her legs firmly around him.

'Get off me,' he cried.

'No! You're mine!'

In desperation, he started to gouge her eyes, pull her hair, anything to extricate himself. She struggled to maintain her grasp and soon only had hold of his hand. Feeling it slip away, she cried out to the gods, 'Gods, help! I beg of you – please ensure we will never be apart!'

The gods, who had been enjoying the spectacle from Mount Olympus, decided to grant her wish – and this is where things really started to get weird.

Despite being almost free of Salmacis, Hermaphroditus was unable to separate his hand from hers. It was as though they were glued together. He tried to force them apart but his skin just stretched and bounced back like rubber. Soon it became impossible to even stretch the skin. Their hands were merging. He noticed that the mole which had been on his thumb was now on hers, and the ring which had been on her finger was now on his – or was that still his thumb and her finger? He could no longer tell the difference. Indeed, after a few seconds there was no difference. Between them, they now only had three hands.

Next their arms fused together, and again their skin started to mix, and so did their muscles, and their veins began coiling round each other, and in one instant it felt as if his bone was being absorbed by hers, and in the next as if hers was being absorbed by his, till eventually they only had three arms between them.

The fusion didn't stop there. It continued across every inch of their bodies – merging tongues, blending eyeballs and two pounding hearts coalescing first in rhythm and then in substance – till only one body remained.

To grant Salmacis's wish that she would never be apart

from Hermaphroditus the gods had united them in flesh and blood.

After the coalescence, how many people is Hermaphroditus? Does Hermaphroditus still exist? Does Salmacis still exist? If you were to kiss Hermaphroditus, how many people would you be kissing?

- If Empedocles was right about metempsychosis, it means that in previous lives you had different parents. If you've had a range of different parents, it follows that your parents in this life aren't essential to your identity. Does this sound right? Could you have had different parents and still be you?
- Inspired by Empedocles's ideas, are these arguments for vegetarianism compelling?

1. Humans and non-human animals are similar.
2. If two things are similar, they should be treated similarly.
3. It is wrong to kill and eat humans.
4. Therefore, it is wrong to kill and eat non-human animals.

1. Murdering the innocent is wrong.
2. Killing animals is murdering the innocent.
3. Therefore, killing animals is wrong.

- Is there an essential difference between humans and non-human animals? Using the following sentence forms below can you think of a definition of 'human being' which is true for *all* humans and *only* humans?

  - 'Creatures that x' (e.g. 'creatures that floss')
  - 'Creatures with x' (e.g. 'creatures with nationalities')

Activities

- According to Empedocles's dualism we are not the same as our bodies. Rather, we are inside our bodies, they are temporary accommodation. But is it possible to think of ourselves in this way? Can we imaginatively alienate ourselves from our bodies? Hold up your hand and wriggle your fingers. Imagine that the hand isn't being controlled by you but is an independent creature moving on its own accord. Are you able to see it in this way?

  Alternatively, lie down on your back and look at your toes. Try to imagine them dissolving into thin air. Now imagine this fade to nothingness continuing to rise up your body, with your legs slowly disappearing, and then your torso, and finally your head, so that all that remains are your disembodied thoughts. Since these thoughts have no body, they presumably also have no location. Is this imaginatively possible? Can you separate your sense of self not only from your current body but from any body whatsoever? Can you think of yourself as not existing in any particular location?

- The ability of all things to coalesce and melt into one is a key part of Empedocles's theory of existence. Let's test whether we are able to experience forms of coalescence. Bang both of your hands down on a table: do the sounds coalesce? Do you hear two separate sounds or one unified sound?

  If you gently stroke the palm of your hand with the tip of the other index finger, do you feel two sensations (touching and being touched) or do the sensations merge into one?

  Use a torch to make shadows with your hand and someone else's. Bring your hands close enough together so that the two shadows begin to overlap. How many shadows are there now? Are you both now casting one shadow?

Or imagine that you and a friend are desert nomads who have each been gifted with canisters of rare and precious water for your birthdays. If one canister of water is poured into the other, how many gifts are there now? Have the two gifts coalesced into one?

Buddha

Questions

- The Buddha believed that human suffering was caused by the impossibility of satisfaction. Does the argument below prove that he was right?

  1. If you want something, then you don't have it.
  2. So if you have it, then you don't want it.
  3. Therefore, we never want what we have.
  4. Therefore, satisfaction is impossible.

- According to the Buddha we do not possess a lasting, enduring self. Beneath our fleeting thoughts and aging bodies there is nothing permanent. Identity is a fiction. This idea has interesting implications for our attitudes towards blame and punishment. If I do not exist, should I be punished for a crime 'I' committed yesterday? The extent to which you believe in the idea of permanent identity may indeed be revealed or determined by your sense of when a person is no longer blameworthy for a past action.

  Imagine that as an 18-year-old you steal a car and manage to get away with it, though only for a time. Consider the various possibilities below for the length of time after the theft before you are identified as the culprit. At which point should you no longer be punished? When are you no longer responsible? When is the act no longer *your* act?

- 1 month later
- 1 year later
- 5 years later
- 10 years later
- 50 years later

- The Buddha is reputed to have said, 'Let, therefore, no man love anything; loss of the beloved is evil. Those who love nothing and hate nothing have no fetters.' Is this wise or foolish?
- According to Buddhist legend, the Buddha remained ignorant of death's reality till the age of 29. Is this believable? If he had never been told about death nor seen anything die, would this make knowledge of death impossible? Or can its reality be inferred from other experiences? Is the experience of pain a memento mori (a sign and reminder of death)? Does vulnerability imply mortality? Does hunger? Is dependence a sign of death? Or is it the case that existence and non-existence are so different that one cannot be logically inferred from the other?

Activities

- The Scottish philosopher David Hume seemed to agree with the Buddha's belief that we have no self when he wrote the following:

> *There are some philosophers, who imagine we are every moment intimately conscious of what we call our SELF; that we feel its existence and its continuance in existence;*

and are certain, beyond the evidence of a demonstration, both of its perfect identity and simplicity...

For my part, when I enter most intimately into what I call myself, I always stumble on some particular perception or other, of heat or cold, light or shade, love or hatred, pain or pleasure. I never can catch myself at any time without a perception, and never can observe any thing but the perception...

I may venture to affirm of the rest of mankind, that they are nothing but a bundle or collection of different perceptions, which succeed each other with an inconceivable rapidity, and are in a perpetual flux and movement. Our eyes cannot turn in their sockets without varying our perceptions. Our thought is still more variable than our sight; and all our other senses and faculties contribute to this change; nor is there any single power of the soul, which remains unalterably the same, perhaps for one moment. The mind is a kind of theatre, where several perceptions successively make their appearance; pass, re-pass, glide away, and mingle in an infinite variety of postures and situations.

Test this out for yourself. Peer inside your mind to see whether you can find *you* within. Beneath the flux of shifting thoughts and feelings do you notice a permanent riverbed? Can you observe a lasting self? Can you find something there that is *having* the thoughts or are thoughts merely happening?

Socrates

Questions

- Socrates believed that bad people cannot have good lives.

For him the sentence, 'I am bad but my life is good,' is contradictory.

Even a hedonist like Aristippus would agree with Socrates on this point: if pleasure is the only good, then to be bad means to be acting against pleasure, which would result in an unpleasurable life, which would not be good. Was Socrates right to regard the idea of a bad person having a good life as an obvious contradiction?

• Socrates also believed that everyone always does what they believe is right, it's just that few people actually know what this is: evil is a kind of stupidity or thoughtlessness. If this is correct, does that mean we should never blame people for their wrongdoing? Certainly, we might wish to condemn their actions, but if they were acting in accordance with their sense of rightness, is it unfair to criticise them for not knowing what this is? Can we fairly condemn or punish people for their ignorance?

• Let's develop Socrates' claim that people who are bad or evil are those who act out of ignorance. Is this convincing?

1. Evil is the total absence of good.
2. If evil is an absence, it is a nothing.
3. It is impossible to think about nothing (because there is nothing to think about).
4. Therefore, it is impossible to think about evil.
5. Therefore, evil people do not think about their actions.

• By refusing to break out of prison before his execution was Socrates behaving foolishly, honourably or both? Was he correct in his belief that we have a duty to the place we come from? Is there anyone, or anything, for whom we should be prepared to die? Is there anyone to whom we owe our lives?

- Socrates believed that there is no point in living unless we are prepared to think about what it means to live well. Was he right? Is it possible to live a good life without knowing what a good life is? If it's possible for animals to have good lives without any knowledge of goodness, is it also possible for us?

Activities

- Have a go at employing Socrates' questioning method (known as the elenchus) to reduce your victim to a state of aporia (perplexity, confusion, uncertainty, annoyance).

1. Find someone in your household.
2. Ask them: What is the most important thing (*x*) in the world?
3. Ask them to define what *x* is, e.g. if they answer 'you', ask, 'What am I?' or if they answer happiness ask, 'What is happiness?'
4. Try to think of an example to show that the definition isn't specific enough.

   For example, if they say, 'You are my child, that is your definition,' you might say, 'My sister is also your child. Does that mean I am my sister?' or, if they say, 'Happiness is having no worries,' you might say, 'Tomatoes have no worries, does that mean they are happy?'
5. Ask them to amend their definition accordingly.
6. Repeat steps 4 and 5 till they give up.
7. Finally, ask them, 'Since you don't even know what *x* is, how can it be important to you?'

Aristippus

Questions

- Do you agree with Aristippus that nothing in the world is better than pleasure? If you stopped being able to feel pleasure, would life be worth living? Contrariwise, is it possible to experience too much pleasure?
- Should we accept Aristippus's view that only the present exists? Consider whether you agree with the following argument:

  1. We can only have what exists.
  2. The past and future don't exist.
  3. Therefore, we have no past or future.

- If only the present exists, it seems important to establish how the long it lasts. Is the time at which you started reading this sentence still part of the present?
- Does the following argument help to clarify the nature of the present?

  1. We are always in the present moment (it is never accurate to say, 'I am in the past,' or 'I am in the future').
  2. If we are always in the present moment, then the present moment doesn't end.
  3. That which doesn't end is infinite.
  4. Therefore, the present moment is infinite.

- If the present is an instantaneous moment without duration, does the following argument prove that we have never seen falling snow:

1. I can only see the present moment. I cannot see what is past.
2. The present moment is instantaneous. It has no duration.
3. Therefore, I can only see what is instantaneous and without duration.
4. Falling snow is a phenomenon with duration. It occurs across instants, not within them.
5. Therefore, I cannot see falling snow.

- Aristippus claimed that it didn't matter whether his girlfriend loved him because being loved doesn't add anything to the pleasure of being kissed. Let's think about this.

  Imagine two people, Simon and Serena. Simon is in a relationship with someone who truly loves him. Serena, unbeknownst to her, is in a relationship with an actor, but one whose performance is flawless and who behaves as affectionately and lovingly as Simon's partner.

  In terms of love, are the lives of Simon and Serena equally good?

- Aristippus believed that as a philosopher his life was more valuable than the lives of non-philosophers. Was he right? When faced with death do some people have more to lose than others?

Activities

- Could you live like Aristippus for a day? Or, less ambitiously, just an hour? Aristippus believed that he had unearthed the essence of a good life: pleasure. Perhaps the only fair and reliable way to assess the truth of this view is to put it into action.

  After conducting your own hedonistic experiment,

consider whether there was anything missing. Did this form of life lack anything vital? Did it lead to any unwanted consequences?

Plato

Questions

- While many of us would now scoff at Plato's argument against democracy, we may share more with his anti-democratic beliefs than we first realise. The UK, for instance, is not a total democracy: prisoners cannot vote, nor can people under the age of 18. Consider the latter point. Why are those under 18 denied the right to vote? What is the justification for this? If it is argued that they are not competent and lack the necessary knowledge and understanding, this reasoning is similar to that which Plato employed to justify his belief that only philosophers should hold political power.

  Are Plato's views, then, simply the logical endpoint of following the reasoning that governments use today to impose age restrictions on voting?

- You have witnessed just actions and seen beautiful sights, but have you ever found justice or beauty themselves? If you haven't and yet still know about these properties, should we conclude that this knowledge does not originate in your experiences of this world? And if you possess knowledge which is not properly of this world, does that show that *you* are not properly of this world? Are you somehow supernatural?

  The above questions take for granted Plato's supposition that there are such things as justice and beauty themselves. But is this correct? Is there something called beauty which is shared by and yet exists over and above beautiful things?

If every beautiful thing in the universe were annihilated, would beauty itself cease to exist?

- Plato believed that education was necessary for fashioning good and just political leaders. Was he right to place such value on the role of education? If it were your responsibility to devise a curriculum for future political leaders, what would you include? Is history necessary? Or art? Or gardening? Or philosophy?

- Plato thought deeply about the question of what makes a good political leader. But rather than question the necessary traits, let's consider whether there are any disqualifying characteristics. For instance, regardless of their policies, would any of the habits and peculiarities described below prevent you from voting for a candidate?

  - She believes in the Tooth Fairy.
  - She sucks her thumb.
  - She eats kittens (doesn't kill them – orders the meat online).
  - She never brushes her teeth.
  - She is homeless (by choice).
  - She crawls instead of walking (by choice).

Activities

- Should we accept Plato's belief that existence is replete with non-physical things? Perhaps we don't even need to investigate the nature of wisdom or beauty to realise their existence. Write down your name on a piece of paper and tear it in two: have you torn your name in two? If not, does that show that names are non-physical things? Now write down one of your beliefs on a piece of paper: if you smell the paper, are you smelling the belief? If not, does that show that beliefs are non-physical things? When you listen to someone speak, are their words entering your body? If not, is this because words are non-physical things? (For more questions on the nature of words flick to the Epicurus questions.)

Diogenes

Questions

• Diogenes believed that we ought to live without shame. If there were a pill that eliminated your capacity to feel embarrassment and shame, would you take it?
• Which of the following do you think you could live without and still have a good life?

  • Money
  • Home
  • Family
  • Comfort
  • Other people's respect
  • Freedom

• As a Cynic Diogenes was not ashamed of going to the toilet in public. But another philosopher St Augustine once argued that the fact that *most* people want privacy when they go to the toilet proves that it is a shameful activity. Was Augustine right?
• Try to imagine what the opposite of Diogenes would be like, the anti-Diogenes, call her Senegoid. Would you prefer to live as Diogenes or Senegoid?
• Inspired by Diogenes's logic when he argued that he was at home in Athens, is the argument below compelling?

1. The universe is my home.
2. The parts of one's home are also one's home.
3. Buckingham Palace is part of the universe.
4. Therefore, Buckingham Palace is my home.

Activities

- Diogenes believed that society forces us to suppress our natural inclinations. How true is this? For one day keep a mental 'Diogenes Diary' noticing every instance in which a consideration of etiquette or politeness changes the way you behave or act.

  What can you conclude from your findings? Is it true that society imposes too many limits on how we behave? Are those restrictions unnatural and therefore irrational? Do you think life would be better without them?

- Diogenes believed that those who complied with social norms did so at the expense of their true human nature; the compliant majority are a pitiful mass of fakes. How easy is it to see the world as he did? Look at the people around you. Imagine that everyone except for you is an actor. Everything they say is scripted. It's all a play, all pretend. Is it easy to adopt this perspective?

  If you look out of the window and spot someone walking their dog, is it possible to see the dog as walking the human? Is it possible to see the humans as the more servile creatures?

  Let's try to take this even further by considering your own authenticity. Can you imagine there's another body inside your body, a person inside you, with arms inside your arms, and legs inside your legs, and a face beneath your face? If so, does this perhaps indicate that there is another, true and natural self within – a self that is trapped within a body of compliance?

Zhuangzi

Questions

- Is it unfair to dismiss the hungry donkey as an ass? Upon reflection was its principle of action genuinely foolish or was its death the result of misapplying its principle? Could it have used its principle to navigate a way out of the dilemma? If so, is there perhaps some wisdom in its rational approach to life? Or was its demise a genuine testament to the limits of using reason to regulate our lives?

- 'The great Way is not named,' wrote Zhuangzi, expressing his belief in the ineffability of reality. But if we cannot understand the Way using words, can we understand it at all? Is it possible to understand anything without language? If this is possible, is it thereby impossible to communicate our understanding with other people? Are there ways of communicating knowledge that don't involve language?

- Imagine a school report for a pupil described by her teachers as aimless, unambitious, undirected and non-committal. Ordinarily, and contrary to Zhuangzi's philosophy, this would be thought of as a damning assessment. But was Zhuangzi right to think that the problem is not with the pupil but our own misguided values? Can you imagine a world in which such a pupil would be lauded and the report framed by her proud parents? What else would have to change about the way we live for us to regard such an assessment favourably? Would you rather live in that world?

Activities

- Can you quieten the mind's tendency to impose order

135

and reason on our experiences? For instance, it's easy enough to make a spoken word lose its meaning by simply repeating it over and over (have a go). But it's harder to make a printed word lose its meaning. Turn your attention to one of the words on this page. Are you able to look at it and see nothing but a meaningless sequence of disconnected shapes?

- Can you similarly quieten the mind's tendency to punctuate our experience of life with aims and goals. Can you cease to will, even briefly? Try to let 10 seconds pass without making a single decision. Is it possible?
- Dreams are the effortless free-flowing stuff of the uninterrupted mind. We don't *make* dreams, we *have* them. They are experiences that happen to us when we relax our control of the mind and let it do its own thing. Our dreaming state therefore approaches the spontaneity of following the Way.

Try to achieve this effortless state of imaginative freedom while awake. Close your eyes and imagine a sycamore seed spinning towards the ground. From this image let your mind wander without guiding it in any particular direction. Allow a phantasmagoria of strange pictures to arise and evolve. Try to have a waking dream.

If you succeed in this, consider what facts cease to be true of you. Are the longings and traits of your waking self also present while you sleep? Think of the Greek hero Odysseus. While asleep was he still homesick? And brave? And Greek? And in love with Penelope? How many dimensions of your identity fade to black with the abeyance of your consciousness?

- To pass through the world free from interference Zhuangzi prescribed attaining a state of empty uselessness. This project starts with ourselves, seeing ourselves as empty, silencing our needs and aims. Experiencing one's own invisibility may facilitate this, and it's easy to achieve: it only requires darkness.

To experience invisibility find a very dark place, a cupboard for instance (you may need to do this at night). Climb into the dark place taking a hand-mirror with you. Hold the mirror up to your face and look at the blackness before you. Keep looking until you start to feel that you are looking at yourself, that you have become the darkness.

- Try to become the happy skull. With one hand under your chin and the other on top of your head, close your eyes and imagine you are holding your own decapitated head.

Pyrrho

Questions

- Pyrrho lived a life free of confusion. He believed this was the key to happiness. If there were a pill that eliminated your capacity to feel confusion, would you take it? To be clear, the pill won't make you omniscient. Rather, though there may still be things you don't know or understand, this won't lead to pangs of confusion. You'll hear extraordinary philosophical questions – 'When you think of a clear sky are your thoughts blue?' or 'When you eat a raspberry are you eating its redness?' or 'Does your voice still exist when you are silent?' or 'Is time invisible?' or 'Can you touch the night?' – but though you may be unsure of the answers, you'll not be befuddled. The uncertainty will never lead to a sense of disquiet or anxiety.
- What is stupider: being stupid or choosing to be stupid?
- Pyrrho seemed to think that all of our beliefs and

judgments depend on our own individual perspectives. Can you think of any facts which don't depend on one's perspective and are absolutely true for everyone?

- Whereas Diogenes was inspired by a mouse, Pyrrho was inspired by a pig. In our approach to life, which animal do you think we should be most inspired by?
- Sceptics like Pyrrho claim that we don't know anything. They think that if you are able to doubt something, then you don't really know it. Since we are able to doubt all of our beliefs we don't really know anything. Let's explore these ideas by testing a range of your beliefs. Let's see whether any of your beliefs are impossible to doubt.

Your age

- How old do you *believe* you are?
- Do you have a good reason for believing this?
- Is there a possibility that you are wrong about this?
- Do you *know* how old you are?

The moon

- Do you *believe* the moon exists?
- Do you have a good reason for believing this?
- Is there a possibility that you are wrong about this?
- Do you *know* that the moon exists?

Your hands

- Do you *believe* you have hands?
- Do you have a good reason for believing this?
- Is there a possibility that you are wrong about this?
- Do you *know* that you have hands?

Your existence

- Do you *believe* that you exist?
- Do you have a good reason for believing this?
- Is there a possibility that you are wrong about this?
- Do you *know* that you exist?

Activities

- Pyrrho wanted to live without beliefs. Try it for yourself. Try to scratch your head and read these words without using or having any beliefs. Is it possible? Is it possible to scratch your head without believing you have a head? Is it possible to read these words without believing they have meaning? Is it possible to breathe without believing in the existence of air or sit without believing in the existence of bums?
- Pyrrho's scepticism partly stemmed from the apparent relativity of all phenomena: facts seem to change as one's perspective changes, and no perspective is more authoritative than any other. Let's test an apparent example of this relativity: lie on the ground and imagine that the sky is beneath you. Imagine that your body is stuck to the ground and that you are looking down at the passing clouds. Is it just as true to say, 'The sky is above me,' as it is, 'The sky is beneath me'?
- Can you meet Pyrrho's challenge of doing something only a sane person would do? If not, would it be reasonable to doubt your sanity?

Epicurus

Questions

- Epicurus believed there was no purpose in nature.

139

Do you agree? Do humans have a purpose? Do chins? Or rocks? Is having a use the same thing as having a purpose? If I use my dog as a footrest, does that mean that is its purpose?

- Are you convinced by the following argument from Epicurus that we shouldn't be troubled by death?

1. If two states are similar, our feelings towards them should be similar.
2. My pre-birth and post-death states of non-existence are similar.
3. I am not saddened by the fact of my pre-birth non-existence.
4. Therefore, I shouldn't be saddened by the fact of my post-death non-existence.

- When the early Christian St Paul travelled to Athens to teach Greek philosophers about the alleged resurrection of Jesus, many of them, including followers of Epicurus, laughed at him. St Paul felt that the story of Jesus's resurrection following his crucifixion was a cause for celebration because it meant that Jesus had managed to overcome death, which St Paul described as our enemy. For Epicurus, on the other hand, since death is the absence of being, and therefore of feeling and sensation, it is 'nothing to us'. His indifference towards death meant that he would have felt no desire to believe in the possibility of resurrection. Which of these stances towards death – as our enemy or as insignificant – do you think is the more realistic? Even if death is a nothing, as Epicurus thought, does that mean it is silly to be troubled by or fear it? Is it unreasonable to fear nothingness?
- The following argument tries to prove that Epicurus was wrong in his belief that we will one day cease to exist. Is

it convincing?

1. If something is possible, then I can imagine it.
2. I cannot imagine my non-existence.
3. Therefore, my non-existence is not possible.

• Epicurus believed that atoms, the building blocks of the universe, are indestructible. Since everything is made of atoms, the universe essentially never becomes emptier. When buildings burn down or reservoirs dry up nothing has really been destroyed. Those particular arrangements of atoms no longer exist, but the atoms themselves will continue forever. Disappearance is merely a matter of atomic rearrangement.

Is Epicurus right that the universe never becomes emptier? When a person dies is there less stuff in the world? Does their death leave an absence? Consider, alternatively, the existence of meaning. Imagine that it's the year 3000. Humans are extinct. All that remains of the species is one solitary copy of *Oliver Twist*. Our cities have turned to dust, our presence on the planet has been erased, except for this one book. Though the pages and printed words remain intact, have their meanings completely disappeared? And if so, is the universe thereby emptier?

• Materialists such as Epicurus believed that the universe is essentially made out of atoms. But if everything is made out of the same stuff – atoms – does that mean that the universe is essentially one thing? Is the apparent diversity of beings a kind of illusion?

And is it really the case that everything in the universe is made of physical stuff? Is this true for words? Consider the word 'sparagmos'. Imagine I burnt every book and deleted every website that used this word. After that I prohibited everyone in the world from saying or thinking about the word for 10 minutes. For those 10 minutes, though the word had no physical form, would it still exist? And if so, does that mean it is not a physical thing?

1. Everything that can be seen can also be smelt.
2. Words cannot be smelt.
3. Therefore, words cannot be seen.

Is this correct? Can words be smelt? If you dig your nose into this book and take a deep sniff, can you smell the words? If they are physical things which can be seen, should this not be a possibility? Or is it perhaps the case that words are not visible, physical things? Is it instead true that when you look at 'sparagmos' you are not looking at a word but the representation of the word?

Activities

• The other side of Epicurus's view that the universe never becomes emptier is that it never becomes fuller. The amount of stuff stays the same. Test this out by passing a sharp pencil through a sheet of paper to 'make' a hole. Have you created something? Is there now something in the world that wasn't there before? If you have created something, does that mean there is now more stuff in the universe?

Blow a raspberry. While creating this sound are you adding to the stuff in existence? Is the universe now fuller? Contrariwise, when you stop, does the universe become emptier?

Clench your hand. Has a new object - a fist - come into existence? Is there now something in the universe that wasn't there before?

Now cup your hands together to create a sort of

dark hollow, leaving an opening at the top so you can look into it. Take a peek, behold the darkness: is it your creation? Has the universe grown in substance with the darkness you've added to it? If you now separate your hands, has the universe lost something? Is it emptier?

Hipparchia

Questions

- Consider the argument Hipparchia used against Theodorus:

  1. Crates and Theodorus are equal.
  2. If two people are equal, then they share the same rights.
  3. Theodorus has the right to slap Theodorus.
  4. Therefore, Crates has the right to slap Theodorus.

  It is certainly clever, but is it correct? For clarity, let's rephrase the argument slightly:

  1. Everyone is equal.
  2. If everyone is equal, then we all share the same rights.
  3. The Queen has the right to slap the Queen.
  4. Therefore, everyone has the right to slap the Queen.

- As a Cynic Hipparchia exhibited a disregard for the norms of society. Does the argument below prove we are free to ignore to such norms, particularly the law?

  1. If there is no law stating that we must do a certain thing, then we are free not to.

2. If there were a law stating that we must follow the law, there would also need to be a law stating that we must follow that law.

3. Premise 2 leads to an infinite regress: that one law would require infinitely more laws to support it.

4. Therefore, there cannot be a law stating that we must follow the law.

5. Therefore, we are free not to follow the law.

- Hipparchia would have rather died than live without autonomy or the fulfilment of her wishes. Similar sentiments were expressed by Seneca when he wrote the following:

> *For mere living is not a good, but living well. Accordingly, the wise man will live as long as he ought, not as long as he can... He always reflects concerning the quality, and not the quantity, of his life. As soon as there are many events in his life that give him trouble and disturb his peace of mind, he sets himself free... He holds that it makes no difference to him whether his departure be natural or self-inflicted, whether it comes later or earlier. He does not regard it with fear, as if it were a great loss; for no man can lose very much when but a driblet remains.*

The Christian philosopher St Augustine, however, had an altogether different view:

> *If you look at the matter closely, you will scarcely call it greatness of soul, which prompts a man to kill himself rather than bear up against some hardships of fortune... Is it not rather proof of a feeble mind, to be unable to bear either the pains of bodily servitude or the foolish opinion of the vulgar? And is not that to be pronounced the greater*

mind, which rather faces than flees the ills of life?

Are you more sympathetic to Hipparchia and Seneca's views on suicide or St Augustine's? Does the willingness to commit suicide in the face of affliction indicate a full or deficient appreciation for the value of life? Is it a sign of strength or weakness? Is it admirable or misguided?

- Hipparchia's preparedness to take her own life was an assertion of self-ownership, a declaration of independence which expressed her belief that it was her life to take. But should we embrace this principle of self-ownership? What, indeed, are the criteria for self-ownership? Do pets, for instance, have self-ownership? Do toddlers? At what point in your life does it become *your* life?

Arguably, you did not gift yourself life, you did not create your life, you did not purchase your life, in many respects you lack control over your life, and others may know more about it than you do. By what right, then, is it yours?

Activities

- Inspired by Hipparchia's ingenious method for mending Theodorus's cloak, let's conduct an experiment. Take a sheet of paper and imagine that this is all you own in the world. Now rip it in two. Have you doubled your possessions?

Jesus

Questions

- Jesus believed that we should aim to be perfect even though it's not humanly possible for us. Do you agree that we should sometimes aim or hope for the impossible? Or should we remain realistic in everything we do and hope for?

Jesus's teachings were a great source of inspiration to the Danish philosopher Søren Kierkegaard. Kierkegaard explored Jesus's ideas about hoping for the impossible through a story about a young man who is in love with a princess. The boy's love for her is vast, his whole life is founded on it, but the two cannot possibly be together (Kierkegaard doesn't tell us why). His wishes are not realistic, reality has nullified them. Kierkegaard proposes three ways the prince might respond.

The first way of responding, Kierkegaard says, is characteristic of 'the frogs in life's swamp.' The frog will adapt to his circumstances and invest his heart in a more realistic love. He will get over it and move on.

The second way of responding belongs to the knight of infinite resignation. This knight will accept the world but refuse to renounce his love. He will resign himself to reality, but he will not temper his love. He will not forget the princess, but love her forever in an abject state of permanent loss. Though the impossibility is accepted, he would rather live in pain than withdraw his heart.

The third way is the knight of faith. Like the knight of infinite resignation he will acknowledge the impossibility of his love whilst holding onto it, he will reconcile himself to the pain. But, unlike the knight of infinite resignation, he will still believe that he can be with the princess. He realises that it isn't merely unlikely, improbable or hard to imagine. He understands that it just can't happen. But he will both resign himself to the impossibility and continue to believe. He will say, 'It is impossible, that is why I believe it, because it is absurd. I will continue to hope though I know that my hope doesn't stand a chance. I will hope because it doesn't stand a chance.'

Whose response do you think is best: the frog's, the knight of infinite resignation's or the knight of faith's?

• Kierkegaard was also deeply moved by Jesus's command that we should love each other, even our enemies, writing 'to love people is the only thing worth living for, and without this love you are not really living'. He believed that when we terminate our love for another person, this is our loss as much as it is theirs:

> *When someone says, 'I have given up my love for this person,' he thinks that it is this person who loses, this person who was the object of his love. The speaker is of the opinion that he himself retains his love in the same sense as someone who has assisted another person with money and says, 'I have stopped giving this assistance to him' – so now the giver keeps the money himself that the other received previously, he who is the loser, since the giver is of course far from losing by this financial shift.*
>
> *But it is not this way with love. Perhaps the one who was the object of love loses, but the one who has 'given up his love for this person,' he is the loser. He perhaps does not detect this himself, perhaps does not even notice that the language mocks him, since he says, 'I have given up my love.' But if he has given up his love, then he has of course given up being loving. Admittedly he adds: my love 'for this person,' but this does not help. With money it can be done this way without loss to oneself, but not with love.*

Kierkegaard believed love only exists through the act of loving, and so, paradoxically, we only acquire love by giving it away. When we cease loving, we lose our love. It is not a commodity.

Do you agree with these ideas? Has he grasped the true nature of love?

- Whereas Jesus longed for and sought perfection, the art critic John Ruskin believed in the greater beauty of imperfection. He wrote:

> *Imperfection is in some sort essential to all that we know of life. It is the sign of life in a mortal body, that is to say, a state of progress and change. Nothing that lives is, or can be, rigidly perfect; part of it is decaying, part nascent... And in all things that live there are certain irregularities and deficiencies which are not only signs of life, but sources of beauty. No human face is exactly the same in its lines on each side, no leaf perfect in its lobe, no branch in its symmetry. All admit irregularity as they imply change; and to banish imperfection is to destroy expression, to check exertion, to paralyse vitality. All things are literally better, lovelier, and more beloved for the imperfections which have been divinely appointed...*

Was Ruskin right? Would the world be poorer without imperfection? If you were faced with two doors, one which led to a perfect world, a world without irregularities, deficiencies, change or decay, and one which led back to our imperfect world, which would you walk through?

- Jesus believed that attaining perfection meant loving everyone – even our enemies – as we love ourselves. But is this possible? Does the argument below prove that it's not?

1. Knowledge is gained from experience.
2. The only life we have fully experienced is our own.
3. Therefore, we can only fully know ourselves.
4. But loving others requires knowing them.
5. Therefore, we can only fully love ourselves.

- In pursuing righteousness Jesus's life and the life of his disciples involved great sacrifice. Is it possible to be a morally excellent person without having a life of sacrifice and hardship? Can a morally excellent person also be comfortable, happy and rich?
- Imagine there were two people who both gave an equal amount of money to a homeless man. The first did so out of love and compassion: she felt saddened by his situation and worried that he wouldn't be able to eat. The second person would have been quite happy if the homeless man had died. She didn't feel any sadness for him and was mostly annoyed by his existence. Nevertheless, she thought it would be wrong to let him starve, so out of a sense of duty she grudgingly gave him money.

  Who was the better person? Given that their actions were identical, were they morally identical? Or was Jesus right to regard our internal thoughts and feelings as no less important than our outward actions?

Activities

- Jesus believed that thoughts can be wrong in themselves. It is, for instance, disloyal for a person to imagine cheating on their partner. It is also disrespectful for children to swear at their parents, even if only in their thoughts.

  Let's test this. Close your eyes and imagine doing something you regard as wrong. It doesn't have to be a horrendous act, just one you would hope never to commit in real life.

  Do you think you just did something wrong? Should we ever be rebuked for our thoughts? Should they be punishable?
- Though we ought to strive for perfection, Jesus thought it was not possible for natural beings such as ourselves

to achieve it. Let's also test this. Are you able to perform any action perfectly? Can you, for instance, walk across the room perfectly? Or read (not recite) these words perfectly? If you cannot be faulted for how you read a word, is it thereby a perfect feat?

You may not have much confidence in your drawing abilities, but could you make a perfectly imperfect drawing of, say, a pineapple?

Seneca

Questions

- Among our repertoire of human traits Seneca thought that anger was responsible for the most suffering. Do you think that any of the traits below have caused more? If you possessed the power of annihilation, which trait (anger included) would you choose to erase from the world?

  - Greed
  - Envy
  - Pride
  - Sloth
  - Lust

- Imagine a philosopher replying to Seneca like so: 'In terms of human suffering, the problem isn't with our emotions or even our actions. The real problem is with power, and the freedom of people in positions of power who, like Nero, can do as they wish. We should not expend our energy trying to fix ourselves but use it to undo the power imbalances that create injustice.' Is this a good objection?

- Seneca said that cruelty is utterly inhuman. But is cruelty always wrong? Is it sometimes fair? Do people ever deserve to be treated cruelly?
- The Scottish philosopher David Hume disagreed with Seneca's views on emotion and reason. Seneca wanted to erase emotion so that our actions could always be motivated by reason. But Hume believed that while reason can guide us, emotion is what makes us act, it's what propels us, and in its absence we'd be motionless (reason without emotion is like a steering wheel without a car). Which philosopher was right?

Activities

- Should you embrace Seneca's views on anger? Rather than reflect on your own actions, it may be easier to find a clear-eyed understanding of the emotion by thinking about the behaviour of other people. Give yourself a few days to observe and study the anger arising in people around you. First of all, as a basic reaction, consider whether you share Seneca's revulsion at what you see. Does the emotion look grotesque?

  Next consider the extent to which the emotion benefited those people. Did it help them overcome their obstacles or satisfy their wishes?

  Finally, ask yourself whether their interests would have been better served without the emotion. Having conducted this brief study into anger, are you sympathetic to Seneca's attitudes towards it? Or did he perhaps fail to notice something of value in the emotion?

Glossary

Atomism *A theory embraced by Epicurus which holds the ontological view that everything in existence is fundamentally composed of physical, indivisible and indestructible entities known as atoms.*

Buddhism *Founded by the Buddha, a religion and system of belief which holds that freedom from suffering is achieved through living a balanced life unburdened by craving and attachment.*

Cynicism *The philosophical theory advanced and exemplified by Diogenes and Hipparchia which claims that in order to be free and happy we ought to abandon the rules and codes of civilisation. Civilisation is unnatural and therefore a lie. We must not allow shame to prevent us from living in accordance with our true nature.*

Daosim *A Chinese school of philosophy which takes its names from the word 'dao', or 'Way'. According to Daoism the universe moves to the spontaneous, non-rational rhythms of the Way, and so should we.*

Dualism *The mind and body are different things. Whereas the body is physical, the mind is non-physical.*

Epistemology *The study of what we can know and how we are able to know it. Scepticism (see below) is an example of an epistemological theory.*

Ethics *The study of how we should live, what we should value and the differences between right and wrong.*

Hedonism *The view held by Aristippus that pleasure is the only and ultimate good in life. An action is not worth doing unless it leads to pleasure. A life without pleasure is worthless.*

Metempsychosis *Also known as reincarnation. The belief that once we have died our souls will enter a different body for the course of another life. Once that life ends, a new body will be found, and so on.*

Ontology *The study of what things exist and what they are like. Ontological questions include: What is reality fundamentally made of? Do non-physical things exist? Is time real? Pythagoras's theory that the world is essentially made of numbers is an example of an ontological theory.*

Whereas epistemology is concerned with questions of what we can know about reality, ontology is concerned with what reality actually is. Platonism (see below) is an example of a theory that consists of both ontological and epistemological claims.

Platonism *A theory instigated and inspired by Plato which holds that the physical, observable world is a mere shadow of a purer, truer, transcendent world. This transcendent world consists of intangible properties – such as beauty, wisdom and justice – whose nature can only be known via the remembrances of our immortal souls.*

Scepticism *The theory exemplified by Pyrrho that knowledge is impossible. Sceptics claim that we do not and cannot know anything.*

Stoicism *The theory inherited by Seneca from ancient Greek philosophers which claims that nature has a rational order and functions in accordance with a divine plan. In our lives we should likewise endeavour to act in accordance with the dictates of reason.*

ACADEMIC AND SPECIALIST

Iff Books publishes non-fiction. It aims to work with authors and titles that augment our understanding of the human condition, society and civilisation, and the world or universe in which we live.
If you have enjoyed this book, why not tell other readers by posting a review on your preferred book site.
Recent bestsellers from Iff Books are:

Why Materialism Is Baloney
How true skeptics know there is no death and fathom answers to life, the universe, and everything
Bernardo Kastrup
A hard-nosed, logical, and skeptic non-materialist metaphysics, according to which the body is in mind, not mind in the body.
Paperback: 978-1-78279-362-5 ebook: 978-1-78279-361-8

The Fall
Steve Taylor
The Fall discusses human achievement versus the issues of war, patriarchy and social inequality.
Paperback: 978-1-78535-804-3 ebook: 978-1-78535-805-0

Brief Peeks Beyond
Critical essays on metaphysics, neuroscience, free will, skepticism and culture
Bernardo Kastrup
An incisive, original, compelling alternative to current mainstream cultural views and assumptions.
Paperback: 978-1-78535-018-4 ebook: 978-1-78535-019-1

Framespotting
Changing how you look at things changes how
you see them
Laurence & Alison Matthews
A punchy, upbeat guide to framespotting. Spot deceptions and
hidden assumptions; swap growth for growing up. See and be free.
Paperback: 978-1-78279-689-3 ebook: 978-1-78279-822-4

Is There an Afterlife?
David Fontana
Is there an Afterlife? If so what is it like? How do Western ideas
of the afterlife compare with Eastern? David Fontana presents the
historical and contemporary evidence for survival of
physical death.
Paperback: 978-1-90381-690-5

Nothing Matters
a book about nothing
Ronald Green
Thinking about Nothing opens the world to everything by
illuminating new angles to old problems and stimulating new
ways of thinking.
Paperback: 978-1-84694-707-0 ebook: 978-1-78099-016-3

Panpsychism
The Philosophy of the Sensuous Cosmos
Peter Ells
Are free will and mind chimeras? This book, anti-materialistic but
respecting science, answers: No! Mind is foundational
to all existence.
Paperback: 978-1-84694-505-2 ebook: 978-1-78099-018-7

Punk Science
Inside the Mind of God
Manjir Samanta-Laughton
Many have experienced unexplainable phenomena; God, psychic
abilities, extraordinary healing and angelic encounters. Can
cutting-edge science actually explain phenomena
previously thought of as 'paranormal'?
Paperback: 978-1-90504-793-2

The Vagabond Spirit of Poetry
Edward Clarke
Spend time with the wisest poets of the modern age and of the
past, and let Edward Clarke remind you of the importance of
poetry in our industrialized world.
Paperback: 978-1-78279-370-0 ebook: 978-1-78279-369-4

Readers of ebooks can buy or view any of these bestsellers by
clicking on the live link in the title. Most titles are published in
paperback and as an ebook. Paperbacks are available in traditional
bookshops. Both print and ebook formats are available online.
Find more titles and sign up to our readers' newsletter at
http://www.johnhuntpublishing.com/non-fiction
Follow us on Facebook at
https://www.facebook.com/JHPNonFiction
and Twitter at https://twitter.com/JHPNonFiction